FOOTBALL LEGENDS

MORTIMER

CONTENTS

DEFENDERS

There are different types of defenders. They cover a range of positions and have different skills. The centre-backs are the big defenders in the middle who mark the opposition strikers. Full-backs operate out wide: they are quick, agile and try to stop wide attackers from crossing balls into the box. Wing-backs play out wide, too, in front of the centre-backs, but also make attacking runs when they have the chance. Finally, the sweeper is the spare defender who is positioned behind the centre-half, ready to help the back four deal with any danger.

WHAT DO THESE STATS MEAN?

75%

AERIAL DUELS WON
This is the percentage of headers a defender has won in his own penalty area, to interrupt an opposition attack.

INTERCEPTIONS
This is the number times a defender has successfully stopped an attack without needing to make a tackle.

BLOCKS
A shot that is intercepted by a defender - preventing his keeper from having to make a save - counts as a block.

KEY PASSES/PASS COMPLETION
A key pass is one that results in an attacking opportunity. Pass completion indicates as a percentage the player's passing accuracy.

CLEARANCES
An attack successfully foiled, either by kicking or heading the ball away from danger, is regarded as a clearance.

TACKLES
This is the number of times a defender has challenged and dispossessed the opposition without committing a foul.

HOW TO USE THIS BOOK

Welcome to *Football Legends* — the exciting book packed with the performance stats of the biggest stars in world of football today! We have chosen more than 100 players and managers from the world's top five leagues: the Bundesliga in Germany, La Liga in Spain, France's Ligue 1, the Italian Serie A and the English Premier League.

You can use this book to figure out who you think the best performers are or you could even get together with friends and play a sort of trading-cards game, comparing the performance records of today's finest defenders, midfielders, forwards, goalkeepers and managers.

The types of stats featured for each position vary, as each position performs a specific role on the pitch. For example, a defender's main job is to stop the opposition from scoring, so the stats focus mainly on this part of their game. Likewise, a striker's tackling is not as relevant as their goal or assists tally. What you will find for all the players is the heat map, which shows how much of the pitch a player covers or, with goalkeepers, whether their strengths lie in the six-yard box or playing as sweeper-keepers who are comfortable all around the penalty area.

The stats span a player's career to date, playing for teams belonging to one of the top five European leagues. The figures have been collected from domestic league and European match appearances only, and exclude data from domestic cup, super cups or international games. This narrow data pool means that the information is instantly comparable so you can decide for yourself who truly deserves to be known as a living legend of the beautiful game.

Did you
know?

For about 40 years from the late 19th century, the most common formation was 2-3-5. It featured only two defenders (right-back and left-back), while the centre-half played in midfield. There were five forwards.

27

NATIONAL TEAM
Austria

CURRENT CLUB
Bayern Munich

DAVID ALABA

David Alaba is amazingly versatile. Best at left-back, he is also skilled with his right foot and can play in central defence, central midfield and as a winger on either flank. His height gives him an aerial advantage and he wins many headers.

BIRTHDATE	24/06/1992
POSITION	FULL-BACK
HEIGHT	1.80 M
WEIGHT	78 KG
PREFERRED FOOT	LEFT

APPEARANCES 336
INTERCEPTIONS 455
BLOCKS 69

AERIAL DUELS WON 50%
PASS COMPLETION 89%

PENALTIES SCORED 3
GOALS 27

KEY PASSES 319
TACKLES 448
CLEARANCES 393

MAJOR CLUB HONOURS
- Bundesliga: x 8 (Between 2011 and 2019)
- UEFA Champions League: 2013
- UEFA Super Cup: 2013
- FIFA Club World Cup: 2013

INTERNATIONAL HONOURS
- None to date

ACTIVITY AREAS

TOBY ALDERWEIRELD

Playing either as a centre-back or right-back, Toby Alderweireld reads the game brilliantly. At his best he is able to anticipate danger, dispossess the opposition with a timely tackle or interception and launch a quick counter-attack.

NATIONAL TEAM
Belgium

CURRENT CLUB
Tottenham Hotspur

BIRTHDATE	02/03/1989
POSITION	CENTRAL
HEIGHT	1.87 M
WEIGHT	90 KG
PREFERRED FOOT	RIGHT

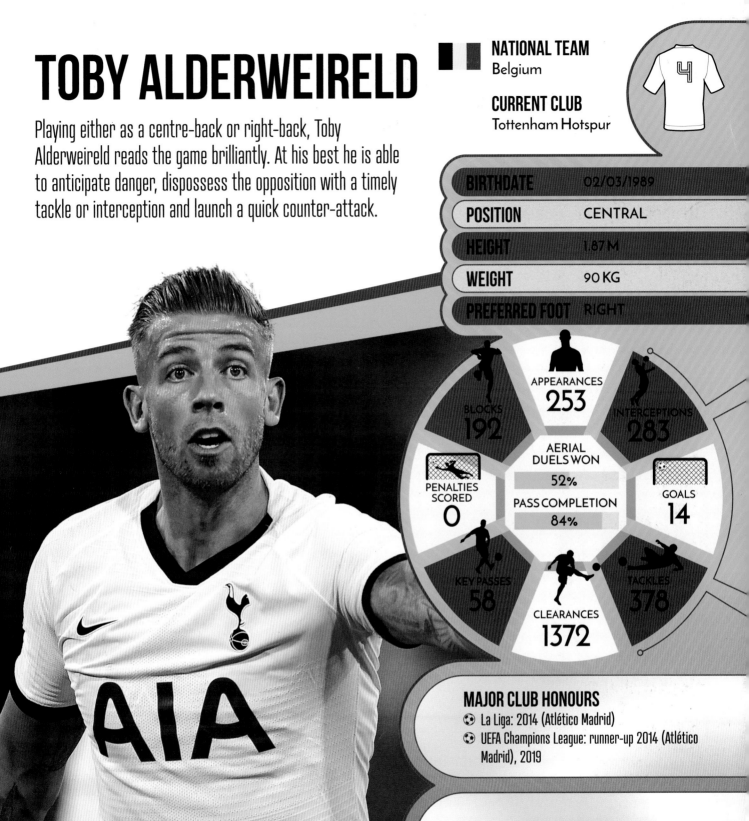

APPEARANCES
253

INTERCEPTIONS
283

BLOCKS
192

AERIAL DUELS WON
52%

PASS COMPLETION
84%

PENALTIES SCORED
0

GOALS
14

KEY PASSES
58

CLEARANCES
1372

TACKLES
378

MAJOR CLUB HONOURS
- La Liga: 2014 (Atlético Madrid)
- UEFA Champions League: runner-up 2014 (Atlético Madrid), 2019

INTERNATIONAL HONOURS
- FIFA World Cup: third place 2018

ACTIVITY AREAS

66

NATIONAL TEAM
England

CURRENT CLUB
Liverpool

TRENT ALEXANDER-ARNOLD

Counted among the world's most exciting young talents, Trent Alexander-Arnold plays at right-back or right wing-back. He is fast, tackles superbly and is capable of whipping in accurate crosses that strikers love to feast on!

BIRTHDATE	07/10/1998
POSITION	FULL-BACK
HEIGHT	1.75 M
WEIGHT	69 KG
PREFERRED FOOT	RIGHT

BLOCKS
20

APPEARANCES
112

INTERCEPTIONS
149

AERIAL DUELS WON
32%

PASS COMPLETION
76%

PENALTIES SCORED
0

GOALS
5

KEY PASSES
193

TACKLES
209

CLEARANCES
223

MAJOR CLUB HONOURS
- UEFA Champions League: 2019
- UEFA Champions League: runner-up 2018
- FIFA Club World Cup: 2019
- UEFA Super Cup: 2019

INTERNATIONAL HONOURS
- UEFA Nations League: third place 2018/19

ACTIVITY AREAS

CÉSAR AZPILICUETA

Right-back César Azpilicueta is a natural leader, who can play anywhere on the pitch. He is excellent at using his positional sense to snuff out danger and frequently starts counter-attacks with a great right foot.

NATIONAL TEAM
Spain

CURRENT CLUB
Chelsea

28

BIRTHDATE	28/08/1989
POSITION	FULL-BACK
HEIGHT	1.78 M
WEIGHT	76 KG
PREFERRED FOOT	RIGHT

APPEARANCES
475

BLOCKS
166

INTERCEPTIONS
967

AERIAL DUELS WON
58%

PENALTIES SCORED
0

PASS COMPLETION
81%

GOALS
12

CLEARANCES
1593

324

1326

MAJOR CLUB HONOURS
- ⚽ Premier League: 2015, 2017
- ⚽ UEFA Europa League: 2015, 2019
- ⚽ FIFA Club World Cup: runner-up 2012

INTERNATIONAL HONOURS
- ⚽ FIFA Confederations Cup: runner-up: 2013

ACTIVITY AREAS

17

NATIONAL TEAM
Germany

CURRENT CLUB
Bayern Munich

JÉRÔME BOATENG

Bayern star defender Jérôme Boateng has proved himself to be one of the best in the business. He is a strong tackler, superb in the air and reads defensive situations excellently, making him a challenge for even the best centre-forwards.

BIRTHDATE	03/09/1988
POSITION	CENTRAL
HEIGHT	1.92 M
WEIGHT	90 KG
PREFERRED FOOT	RIGHT

APPEARANCES
382

BLOCKS
132

INTERCEPTIONS
672

AERIAL DUELS WON
66%

PASS COMPLETION
85%

PENALTIES SCORED
0

GOALS
8

KEY PASSES
190

CLEARANCES
1155

TACKLES
681

MAJOR CLUB HONOURS
⚽ Bundesliga: 2013, 2014, 2015, 2016, 2017, 2018, 2019 ⚽ UEFA Champions League: 2013 ⚽ UEFA Champions League: runner-up 2018 ⚽ FIFA Club World Cup: 2013 ⚽ UEFA Super Cup: 2013

INTERNATIONAL HONOURS
⚽ FIFA World Cup: 2014

ACTIVITY AREAS

LEONARDO BONUCCI

Italy's vice captain Leonardo Bonucci is a strong and experienced centre-back with exceptional ball skills. He is superb at breaking up play and launching attacks with long passes. What's more, he poses a goal threat from set pieces.

NATIONAL TEAM
Italy

CURRENT CLUB
Juventus

19

BIRTHDATE	01/05/1987
POSITION	CENTRAL
HEIGHT	1.90 M
WEIGHT	85 KG
PREFERRED FOOT	RIGHT

APPEARANCES
439

BLOCKS
271

INTERCEPTIONS
780

AERIAL DUELS WON
54%

PASS COMPLETION
86%

PENALTIES SCORED
0

GOALS
25

KEY PASSES
133

CLEARANCES
1933

TACKLES
546

MAJOR CLUB HONOURS
- Serie A: 2006 (Inter Milan), 2012, 2013, 2014, 2015, 2016, 2017, 2019
- Coppa Italia: 2015, 2016, 2017

INTERNATIONAL HONOURS
- UEFA European Championship: runner-up 2012
- FIFA Confederations Cup: third place 2013

ACTIVITY AREAS

3

GEORGIO CHIELLINI

The Italian is a hard-tackling centre-back whose no-nonsense approach to winning the ball makes him tough to beat. He can also play as an emergency attacker and is famous for beating his chest in celebration whenever he scores.

BIRTHDATE	14/08/1984
POSITION	CENTRAL
HEIGHT	1.87 M
WEIGHT	85 KG
PREFERRED FOOT	LEFT

APPEARANCES
474

BLOCKS
252

INTERCEPTIONS
1440

AERIAL DUELS WON
67%

PASS COMPLETION
84%

PENALTIES SCORED
0

GOALS
31

KEY PASSES
230

CLEARANCES
3077

TACKLES
1276

MAJOR CLUB HONOURS
- ⚽ Serie A: 2012, 2013, 2014, 2015, 2016, 2017, 2019
- ⚽ Coppa Italia: 2015, 2016, 2017, 2018

INTERNATIONAL HONOURS
- ⚽ Olympic Games: bronze medal 2004

ACTIVITY AREAS

VIRGIL VAN DIJK

Dutch captain Virgil van Dijk's pace, power, passing and aerial ability have made him into one of the finest centre-backs in the world. He is also blessed with a sweet right foot and is a lethal free-kick specialist.

NATIONAL TEAM
Netherlands

CURRENT CLUB
Liverpool

BIRTHDATE	08/07/1991
POSITION	CENTRAL
HEIGHT	1.93 M
WEIGHT	92 KG
PREFERRED FOOT	RIGHT

APPEARANCES
194

BLOCKS
103

INTERCEPTIONS
355

PENALTIES SCORED
0

AERIAL DUELS WON
73%

PASS COMPLETION
87%

GOALS
16

KEY PASSES
51

CLEARANCES
1154

TACKLES
225

MAJOR CLUB HONOURS
- ⚽ Scottish Premier League: 2014, 2015 (Celtic)
- ⚽ UEFA Champions League: 2019
- ⚽ FIFA Club World Cup: 2019
- ⚽ UEFA Super Cup: 2019

INTERNATIONAL HONOURS
- ⚽ UEFA Nations League: runner-up 2019

ACTIVITY AREAS

15

2

NATIONAL TEAM
Uruguay

CURRENT CLUB
Atlético Madrid

JOSÉ GIMÉNEZ

The Uruguayan is a tough-tackling centre-back who is quick off the mark and difficult to knock off the ball. He made his international debut when he was just 19 and has also thrived at club level since joining Atlético Madrid in 2013.

BIRTHDATE	20/01/1995
POSITION	CENTRAL
HEIGHT	1.85 M
WEIGHT	80 KG
PREFERRED FOOT	RIGHT

BLOCKS
99

APPEARANCES
158

INTERCEPTIONS
325

AERIAL DUELS WON
67%

PASS COMPLETION
79%

PENALTIES SCORED
0

GOALS
5

KEY PASSES
34

CLEARANCES
776

TACKLES
288

MAJOR CLUB HONOURS
- ⚽ UEFA Europa League: 2018
- ⚽ UEFA Super Cup: 2018
- ⚽ UEFA Champions League: runner-up 2014, 2016

INTERNATIONAL HONOURS
- ⚽ China Cup: 2018, 2019

ACTIVITY AREAS

DIEGO GODÍN

Diego Godín is a top-class centre-half who has been one of the most rock-solid defenders in Europe over the past decade. He uses his superb positional sense to make crucial tackles and often marks the best attackers.

NATIONAL TEAM
Uruguay

CURRENT CLUB
Inter Milan

2

BIRTHDATE	16/02/1986
POSITION	CENTRAL
HEIGHT	1.87 M
WEIGHT	78 KG
PREFERRED FOOT	RIGHT

APPEARANCES
479

BLOCKS
228

INTERCEPTIONS
1226

AERIAL DUELS WON
67%

PENALTIES SCORED
0

PASS COMPLETION
79%

GOALS
27

KEY PASSES
98

TACKLES
1030

CLEARANCES
3032

MAJOR CLUB HONOURS

⚽ La Liga: 2014 (Atlético Madrid) ⚽ UEFA Europa League: 2012, 2018 (Atlético Madrid) ⚽ UEFA Super Cup: 2010, 2012, 2018 (Atlético Madrid)

INTERNATIONAL HONOURS

⚽ Copa América: 2011
⚽ China Cup: 2018, 2019

ACTIVITY AREAS

NATIONAL TEAM
Germany

CURRENT CLUB
Borussia Dortmund

MATS HUMMELS

The German is regarded as one of the best ball-playing defenders on the planet. Hummels can physically tussle with the strongest of forwards, but it is his ability to stride forward and set up attacks with his fine passing that sets him apart.

BIRTHDATE	16/12/1988
POSITION	CENTRAL
HEIGHT	1.91 M
WEIGHT	94 KG
PREFERRED FOOT	RIGHT

BLOCKS
152

APPEARANCES
398

INTERCEPTIONS
925

AERIAL DUELS WON
67%

PASS COMPLETION
83%

PENALTIES SCORED
1

GOALS
29

KEY PASSES
151

CLEARANCES
1695

TACKLES
977

MAJOR CLUB HONOURS
⚽ Bundesliga: 2011, 2012, 2017, 2018, 2019
⚽ DFB-Pokal: 2012, 2019

INTERNATIONAL HONOURS
⚽ UEFA Champions League: runner-up 2013
⚽ FIFA World Cup: 2014

ACTIVITY AREAS

KALIDOU KOULIBALY

Kalidou Koulibaly is an aggressive centre-back, perfect for his side's high-pressing game. Extremely fast, he is capable of sprinting back to cover even if the opposition play the ball over the top or in behind his team's high defensive line.

NATIONAL TEAM
Senegal

CURRENT CLUB
Napoli

26

BIRTHDATE	20/06/1991
POSITION	CENTRAL
HEIGHT	1.87 M
WEIGHT	89 KG
PREFERRED FOOT	RIGHT

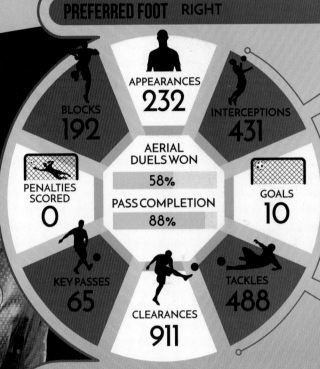

APPEARANCES
232

BLOCKS
192

INTERCEPTIONS
431

PENALTIES SCORED
0

AERIAL DUELS WON
58%

PASS COMPLETION
88%

GOALS
10

KEY PASSES
65

CLEARANCES
911

TACKLES
488

MAJOR CLUB HONOURS
- Belgian Cup: 2013 (Genk)
- Supercoppa Italiana: 2014

INTERNATIONAL HONOURS
- None to date

ACTIVITY AREAS

19

NATIONAL TEAM
France

CURRENT CLUB
Manchester City

AYMERIC LAPORTE

Aymeric Laporte has become one of Europe's best central defenders. Very strong, he is powerful in the tackle, excellent in the air and a good organiser at the back. Laporte can also start attacks with his precise passing out of defence.

BIRTHDATE	27/05/1994
POSITION	CENTRAL
HEIGHT	1.91 M
WEIGHT	86 KG
PREFERRED FOOT	LEFT

APPEARANCES
256

BLOCKS
107

INTERCEPTIONS
572

AERIAL DUELS WON
65%

PENALTIES SCORED
0

PASS COMPLETION
86%

GOALS
12

KEY PASSES
65

CLEARANCES
1043

TACKLES
480

MAJOR CLUB HONOURS
⚽ Supercopa de España: 2015 (Athletic Bilbao)
⚽ Premier League: 2018, 2019

INTERNATIONAL HONOURS
⚽ UEFA European U-19 Championship: runner-up 2013

ACTIVITY AREAS

HARRY MAGUIRE

Harry Maguire attended a EURO 2016 match as a fan and only two years later played for England at the 2018 World Cup. He is a technically gifted centre-back, superb in the air, a strong tackler and very capable with the ball at his feet.

NATIONAL TEAM
England

CURRENT CLUB
Manchester United

BIRTHDATE	05/03/1993
POSITION	CENTRAL
HEIGHT	1.94 M
WEIGHT	100 KG
PREFERRED FOOT	RIGHT

APPEARANCES
136

BLOCKS
92

INTERCEPTIONS
218

AERIAL DUELS WON
72%

PASS COMPLETION
82%

PENALTIES SCORED
0

GOALS
8

KEY PASSES
54

CLEARANCES
633

TACKLES
191

MAJOR CLUB HONOURS
⚽ Football League Championship: play-offs 2016 (Hull City)

INTERNATIONAL HONOURS
⚽ UEFA Nations League: third place 2019

ACTIVITY AREAS

5

NATIONAL TEAM
Brazil

CURRENT CLUB
Paris Saint-Germain

MARQUINHOS

Marquinhos is a clever defender. He may not be a powerhouse like many of today's top-class centre-backs, but has the speed, agility and intelligence to mark the quickest forwards, plus he can be very effective going forward.

BIRTHDATE	14/05/1994
POSITION	CENTRAL
HEIGHT	1.83 M
WEIGHT	75 KG
PREFERRED FOOT	RIGHT

APPEARANCES
257

BLOCKS
151

INTERCEPTIONS
414

AERIAL DUELS WON
58%

PENALTIES SCORED
0

PASS COMPLETION
92%

GOALS
18

KEY PASSES
50

CLEARANCES
951

TACKLES
436

MAJOR CLUB HONOURS
⚽ Ligue 1: 2014, 2015, 2016, 2018, 2019
⚽ Coupe de France: 2015, 2016, 2017, 2018

INTERNATIONAL HONOURS
⚽ Copa América: 2019

ACTIVITY AREAS

BENJAMIN PAVARD

One of the stars to emerge at the 2018 World Cup, Benjamin Pavard has since matured into a technically brilliant defender at Bayern Munich. He is usually in the right place at the right time to tackle or intercept dangerous passes.

NATIONAL TEAM
France

CURRENT CLUB
Bayern Munich

BIRTHDATE	28/03/1996.
POSITION	CENTRAL
HEIGHT	1.86 M
WEIGHT	76 KG
PREFERRED FOOT	RIGHT

APPEARANCES
114

BLOCKS
66

INTERCEPTIONS
209

AERIAL DUELS WON
57%

PENALTIES SCORED
00

PASS COMPLETION
86%

GOALS
3

KEY PASSES
46

CLEARANCES
476

TACKLES
133

MAJOR CLUB HONOURS
⚽ Bundesliga: 2017

INTERNATIONAL HONOURS
⚽ FIFA World Cup: 2018

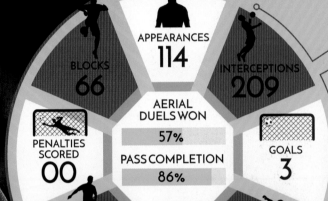

ACTIVITY AREAS

NATIONAL TEAM
Spain

CURRENT CLUB
Barcelona

GERARD PIQUÉ

Gerard Piqué is still classed among the best defenders in the world. Normally a centre-half, he can also play at sweeper or in front of the defence. He is an accurate passer, plus his height gives him an aerial advantage over his opponents.

BIRTHDATE	02/02/1987
POSITION	CENTRAL
HEIGHT	1.94 M
WEIGHT	85 KG
PREFERRED FOOT	RIGHT

BLOCKS
251

APPEARANCES
484

INTERCEPTIONS
706

AERIAL DUELS WON
65%

PASS COMPLETION
89%

PENALTIES SCORED
0

GOALS
44

KEY PASSES
83

TACKLES
777

CLEARANCES
2144

MAJOR CLUB HONOURS
⚽ La Liga: 2009, 2010, 2011, 2013, 2015, 2016, 2018, 2019 ⚽ UEFA Champions League: 2008, 2009, 2011, 2015 ⚽ UEFA Super Cup: 2009, 2015 ⚽ FIFA Club World Cup: 2009, 2011, 2015

INTERNATIONAL HONOURS
⚽ FIFA World Cup: 2010
⚽ UEFA European Championship: 2012

ACTIVITY AREAS

SERGIO RAMOS

Centre-back Sergio Ramos has been a star at Real Madrid ever since he joined the club in 2005. Not only is he a skilled defender and great team leader, but is also known for regularly scoring important goals for his team.

NATIONAL TEAM
Spain

CURRENT CLUB
Real Madrid

BIRTHDATE	30/03/1986
POSITION	CENTRAL
HEIGHT	1.84 M
WEIGHT	82 KG
PREFERRED FOOT	RIGHT

APPEARANCES
607

BLOCKS
291

INTERCEPTIONS
1389

AERIAL DUELS WON
68%

PASS COMPLETION
87%

PENALTIES SCORED
12

GOALS
79

KEY PASSES
275

TACKLES
1292

CLEARANCES
2589

MAJOR CLUB HONOURS
⚽ La Liga: 2007, 2008, 2012, 2017 ⚽ UEFA Champions League: 2014, 2016, 2017, 2018 ⚽ UEFA Super Cup: 2014, 2016, 2017 ⚽ FIFA Club World Cup: 2014, 2016, 2017

INTERNATIONAL HONOURS
⚽ FIFA World Cup: 2010
⚽ UEFA European Championship: 2008, 2012
⚽ FIFA Confederations Cup: third place 2009, runner-up 2013

ACTIVITY AREAS

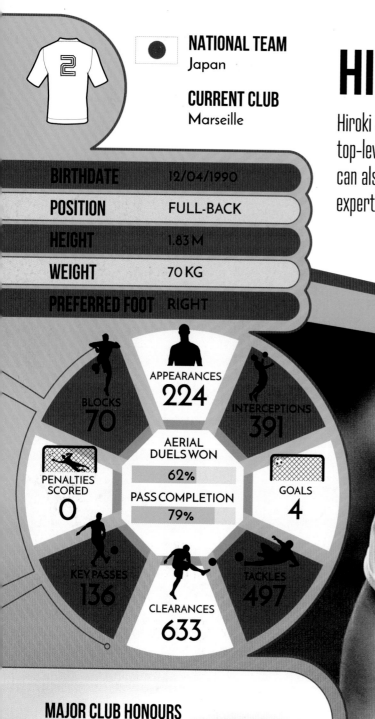

NATIONAL TEAM
Japan

CURRENT CLUB
Marseille

HIROKI SAKAI

Hiroki Sakai is one of the few Japanese defenders to play top-level European club football. Normally a right-back, Sakai can also adapt his game to play in other positions. He is an expert ball-winner who is fast and always alert to danger.

BIRTHDATE	12/04/1990
POSITION	FULL-BACK
HEIGHT	1.83 M
WEIGHT	70 KG
PREFERRED FOOT	RIGHT

APPEARANCES
224

BLOCKS
70

INTERCEPTIONS
391

AERIAL DUELS WON
62%

PENALTIES SCORED
0

PASS COMPLETION
79%

GOALS
4

KEY PASSES
136

CLEARANCES
633

TACKLES
497

MAJOR CLUB HONOURS
⚽ UEFA Europa League: runner-up 2018

INTERNATIONAL HONOURS
⚽ AFC Asian Cup: runner-up 2019

ACTIVITY AREAS

26

THIAGO SILVA

Players past and present rate Thiago Silva as one of the best-ever central defenders to play the game. In addition to his technical strengths, he is a natural leader who is able to inspire team-mates to raise their game in the heat of battle.

NATIONAL TEAM
Brazil

CURRENT CLUB
Paris Saint-Germain

BIRTHDATE	22/09/1984
POSITION	CENTRAL
HEIGHT	1.83 M
WEIGHT	79 KG
PREFERRED FOOT	RIGHT

APPEARANCES
374

BLOCKS
254

INTERCEPTIONS
873

AERIAL DUELS WON
72%

PASS COMPLETION
93%

PENALTIES SCORED
0

GOALS
18

KEY PASSES
84

CLEARANCES
2068

TACKLES
598

MAJOR CLUB HONOURS
- ⚽ Serie A: 2011 (AC Milan)
- ⚽ Ligue 1: 2013, 2014, 2015, 2016, 2018, 2019
- ⚽ Coupe de la Ligue: 2014, 2015, 2016, 2017, 2018

INTERNATIONAL HONOURS
- ⚽ FIFA Confederations Cup; 2013
- ⚽ Copa América: 2019

ACTIVITY AREAS

27

37

NATIONAL TEAM
Slovakia

CURRENT CLUB
Inter Milan

MILAN ŠKRINIAR

Centre-back Milan Škriniar is a forceful tackler, strong in the air and combative on the ground. But what sets Škriniar apart are his ball-playing skills and ability to stay calm under pressure and pick out intelligent passes.

BIRTHDATE	11/02/1995
POSITION	CENTRAL
HEIGHT	1.87 M
WEIGHT	80 KG
PREFERRED FOOT	LEFT

APPEARANCES 150
BLOCKS 99
INTERCEPTIONS 157
AERIAL DUELS WON 54%
PASS COMPLETION 92%
PENALTIES SCORED 0
GOALS 4
KEY PASSES 30
CLEARANCES 605
TACKLES 265

MAJOR CLUB HONOURS
⚽ Slovak Super Liga: 2012 (MŠK Žilina)
⚽ Slovak Cup: 2012 (MŠK Žilina)

INTERNATIONAL HONOURS
⚽ King's Cup: 2018

ACTIVITY AREAS

DAYOT UPAMECANO

This rising star has blistering pace which helps him to make important tackles, interceptions and win headers. But Upamecano's standout talent is his ability with the ball at his feet — a quality that complements his passing accuracy.

NATIONAL TEAM
France

CURRENT CLUB
RB Leipzig

BIRTHDATE	27/10/1998
POSITION	CENTRAL
HEIGHT	1.86 M
WEIGHT	90 KG
PREFERRED FOOT	RIGHT

BLOCKS
44

APPEARANCES
101

INTERCEPTIONS
195

AERIAL DUELS WON
62%

PASS COMPLETION
85%

PENALTIES SCORED
0

GOALS
3

KEY PASSES
26

CLEARANCES
407

TACKLES
218

MAJOR CLUB HONOURS
⚽ None to date

INTERNATIONAL HONOURS
⚽ UEFA European Under-17 Championship: 2015

ACTIVITY AREAS

 NATIONAL TEAM
France

CURRENT CLUB
Real Madrid

RAPHAËL VARANE

While most defenders shine in their late 20s, Raphaël Varane was already a star in his teens. Accurate with either foot, an excellent tackler and great in the air, Varane can also launch attacks with his sharp passing and even score goals.

BIRTHDATE	25/04/1993
POSITION	CENTRAL
HEIGHT	1.91 M
WEIGHT	81 KG
PREFERRED FOOT	RIGHT

APPEARANCES
292

INTERCEPTIONS
446

BLOCKS
146

AERIAL DUELS WON
69%

PASS COMPLETION
88%

PENALTIES SCORED
0

GOALS
10

KEY PASSES
49

CLEARANCES
1350

TACKLES
367

MAJOR CLUB HONOURS
- La Liga: 2012, 2017
- UEFA Champions League: 2014, 2016, 2017, 2018
- UEFA Super Cup: 2014, 2016, 2017
- FIFA Club World Cup: 2014, 2016, 2017, 2018

INTERNATIONAL HONOURS
- FIFA World Cup: 2018

ACTIVITY AREAS

JAN VERTONGHEN

Jan Vertonghen's leadership holds together the defence of his teams both at club and national levels. Normally a left-footed centre-half, he also plays at left-back. He is good in the air, reads the game well and wins important challenges.

NATIONAL TEAM
Belgium

CURRENT CLUB
Tottenham Hotspur

BIRTHDATE	24/04/1987
POSITION	CENTRAL
HEIGHT	1.89 M
WEIGHT	87 KG
PREFERRED FOOT	LEFT

APPEARANCES
307

BLOCKS
144

INTERCEPTIONS
625

AERIAL DUELS WON
69%

PASS COMPLETION
87%

PENALTIES SCORED
0

GOALS
9

KEY PASSES
100

CLEARANCES
1698

TACKLES
589

MAJOR CLUB HONOURS
- Eredivisie: 2011, 2012 (Ajax)
- UEFA Champions League: runner-up 2019

INTERNATIONAL HONOURS
- FIFA World Cup: third place 2018

ACTIVITY AREAS

31

MIDFIELDERS

Midfielders are the heartbeat of a team. Not only do they play between the forwards and the defenders, but they also help out their team-mates at both ends. Midfielders fall into one of four main categories: 1) defensive midfielders, who sit in front of the back four and are great tacklers; 2) the attacking full-backs operating on the wings who whip crosses into the box; 3) the central midfielders who are brilliant at setting up and then joining attacks, as well as helping out in defence whenever needed; 4) the playmakers — these are stars who build the attack with their creative play.

WHAT DO THE STATS MEAN?

ASSISTS
A pass, cross or header to a team-mate who then scores counts as an assist. This stat also includes a deflected shot that is converted by a team-mate.

SHOTS
Any deliberate strike on goal counts as a shot. The strike does not have to be on target or force a save from the keeper.

CHANCES CREATED
Any pass that results in a shot at goal (whether or not the goal is scored) is regarded as a chance created.

TACKLES
This is the number of times the player has challenged and dispossessed the opposition without committing a foul.

DRIBBLES
This is the number of times the player has gone past an opponent while running with the ball.

75%

SUCCESSFUL PASSES
This shows as a percentage how successful the midfielder is at finding team-mates with passes, whether over five or 60 yards.

Did you know?

In top-level football, midfielders tend to cover the most ground during the course of a match. A midfielder playing the full 90 minutes will usually run anywhere between 9.5 and 12km.

11

 NATIONAL TEAM
Wales

CURRENT CLUB
Real Madrid

GARETH BALE

Gareth Bale started his career as a full-back before developing into an attacking player. Lightning quick and with a sweet left foot, he is a constant threat up front and is known for scoring spectacular long-range goals.

BIRTHDATE	16/07/1989
POSITION	WINGER
HEIGHT	1.85 M
WEIGHT	81 KG
PREFERRED FOOT	LEFT

ASSISTS
79

APPEARANCES
398

DRIBBLES
1500

PENALTIES
SCORED
3

PASSES
11530
SUCCESSFUL
PASSES
77.9%

GOALS
145

SHOTS
1174

CHANCES
CREATED
622

TACKLES
411

MAJOR CLUB HONOURS
⚽ UEFA Champions League: 2014, 2016, 2017, 2018
⚽ UEFA Super Cup: 2014, 2016, 2017
⚽ FIFA Club World Cup: 2014, 2017, 2018

INTERNATIONAL HONOURS
⚽ None to date

ACTIVITY AREAS

KEVIN DE BRUYNE

Kevin De Bruyne ranks as one of the finest attacking midfielders in the game today. Strong and technically brilliant, he can break up play at one end and almost immediately blast a 25-metre shot into the opposite goal.

NATIONAL TEAM
Belgium

CURRENT CLUB
Manchester City

BIRTHDATE	28/06/1991
POSITION	ATTACKING
HEIGHT	1.81 M
WEIGHT	68 KG
PREFERRED FOOT	RIGHT

APPEARANCES
282

ASSISTS
113

DRIBBLES
940

PENALTIES SCORED
1

PASSES
14027
SUCCESSFUL PASSES
79.9%

GOALS
65

SHOTS
663

CHANCES CREATED
805

TACKLES
357

MAJOR CLUB HONOURS
⚽ Premier League: 2018, 2019
⚽ FA Cup: 2019

INTERNATIONAL HONOURS
⚽ FIFA World Cup: third place 2018

ACTIVITY AREAS

35

NATIONAL TEAM
Spain

CURRENT CLUB
Barcelona

SERGIO BUSQUETS

Sergio Busquets plays as a deep midfielder who dictates the team's build-up play with clever, short and longer passes. He is great at stopping attacks before they become dangerous and then making passes to launch his team's raids.

BIRTHDATE	16/07/1988
POSITION	DEFENSIVE
HEIGHT	1.89 M
WEIGHT	76 KG
PREFERRED FOOT	RIGHT

ASSISTS
31

APPEARANCES
481

DRIBBLES
363

PASSES
34660

SUCCESSFUL PASSES
91.0%

PENALTIES SCORED
0

GOALS
13

SHOTS
112

CHANCES CREATED
284

TACKLES
1298

MAJOR CLUB HONOURS
⚽ UEFA Champions League: 2009, 2011, 2015
⚽ UEFA Super Cup: 2009, 2011, 2015
⚽ FIFA Club World Cup: 2009, 2011, 2015

INTERNATIONAL HONOURS
⚽ FIFA World Cup: 2010
⚽ UEFA European Championship: 2012
⚽ FIFA Confederations Cup: third place 2009, runner-up 2013

ACTIVITY AREAS

EMRE CAN

Having been a defender earlier in his career, Emre Can has grown into a classy central midfielder. He combines his excellent tackling strength with his midfielder's instincts to thread passes to team-mates in attacking positions.

NATIONAL TEAM
Germany

CURRENT CLUB
Borussia Dortmund*

*On loan from Juventus

BIRTHDATE	12/01/1994
POSITION	CENTRAL
HEIGHT	1.84 M
WEIGHT	82 KG
PREFERRED FOOT	RIGHT

APPEARANCES
231

ASSISTS
12

DRIBBLES
463

PENALTIES SCORED
1

PASSES
10918
SUCCESSFUL PASSES
83.1%

GOALS
21

SHOTS
241

CHANCES CREATED
166

TACKLES
552

MAJOR CLUB HONOURS
⚽ Bundesliga: 2013 (Bayern Munich) ⚽ UEFA Champions League: 2013 (Bayern Munich), runner-up 2018 (Liverpool) ⚽ UEFA Europa League: runner-up 2016 (Liverpool) ⚽ Serie A: 2019 (Juventus)

INTERNATIONAL HONOURS
⚽ FIFA Confederations Cup: 2017

ACTIVITY AREAS

NATIONAL TEAM
Brazil

CURRENT CLUB
Bayern Munich*

*On loan from Barcelona

PHILIPPE COUTINHO

Philippe Coutinho brings Brazilian flair to the pitch whenever he plays. Highly skilled with both feet, he is the type of attacking midfielder opposition defenders hate to face. Coutinho scores an average of one goal every four games.

BIRTHDATE	12/06/1992
POSITION	ATTACKING
HEIGHT	1.72 M
WEIGHT	68 KG
PREFERRED FOOT	RIGHT

APPEARANCES
327

ASSISTS
61

DRIBBLES
1267

PASSES
12798

SUCCESSFUL PASSES
81.9%

PENALTIES SCORED
2

GOALS
82

SHOTS
905

CHANCES CREATED
531

TACKLES
401

MAJOR CLUB HONOURS
- La Liga: 2018, 2019 (Barcelona)
- Copa del Rey: 2018 (Barcelona)

INTERNATIONAL HONOURS
- FIFA Under-20 World Cup: 2011
- Copa América: 2019

ACTIVITY AREAS

JULIAN DRAXLER

Julian Draxler is a thrill to watch! He has the pace to get past the defence and deliver a dangerous cross or pass with pinpoint accuracy. If going for goal himself, he is capable of an impressive left-footed strike.

NATIONAL TEAM
Germany

CURRENT CLUB
Paris Saint-Germain

23

BIRTHDATE	20/09/1993
POSITION	ATTACKING
HEIGHT	1.85 M
WEIGHT	72 KG
PREFERRED FOOT	RIGHT

APPEARANCES
304

DRIBBLES
1052

ASSISTS
44

PENALTIES SCORED
0

PASSES
10160

SUCCESSFUL PASSES
86.1%

GOALS
43

SHOTS
424

CHANCES CREATED
395

TACKLES
307

MAJOR CLUB HONOURS
⚽ Ligue 1: 2018, 2019
⚽ Coupe de France: 2017, 2018

INTERNATIONAL HONOURS
⚽ FIFA World Cup: 2014
⚽ FIFA Confederations Cup: 2017

ACTIVITY AREAS

24

NATIONAL TEAM
Denmark

CURRENT CLUB
Inter Milan

CHRISTIAN ERIKSEN

Christian Eriksen has a great footballing brain which allows him to be a key player as a No.10, or central midfielder. He is excellent at setting up chances for his forwards or scoring with his dangerous right foot, especially free-kicks.

BIRTHDATE	14/02/1992
POSITION	ATTACKING
HEIGHT	1.82 M
WEIGHT	76 KG
PREFERRED FOOT	BOTH

ASSISTS
83

APPEARANCES
309

DRIBBLES
549

PASSES
15527

SUCCESSFUL
PASSES
81.7%

PENALTIES
SCORED
0

GOALS
65

SHOTS
749

CHANCES
CREATED
765

TACKLES
357

MAJOR CLUB HONOURS
⚽ Eredivisie: 2011, 2012, 2013 (Ajax)
⚽ UEFA Champions League: runner-up 2019
(Tottenham Hotspur)

INTERNATIONAL HONOURS
⚽ None to date

ACTIVITY AREAS

FABINHO

After a slow start to his Liverpool career, Fabinho has now become a fan favourite. Tall and strong, he is a master at keeping possession for his team and starting the attack from deep. His heat map shows how dominant he is in midfield.

NATIONAL TEAM
Brazil

CURRENT CLUB
Liverpool

BIRTHDATE	23/10/1993
POSITION	DEFENSIVE
HEIGHT	1.88 M
WEIGHT	78 KG
PREFERRED FOOT	RIGHT

ASSISTS
16

APPEARANCES
264

DRIBBLES
370

PENALTIES SCORED
17

PASSES
12868
SUCCESSFUL PASSES
83.5%

GOALS
27

SHOTS
162

CHANCES CREATED
186

TACKLES
740

MAJOR CLUB HONOURS
⚽ Ligue 1: 2017 (Monaco)
⚽ UEFA Champions League: 2019
⚽ UEFA Super Cup: 2019

INTERNATIONAL HONOURS
⚽ Superclásico de las Américas: 2018

ACTIVITY AREAS

41

NATIONAL TEAM
Brazil

CURRENT CLUB
Liverpool

ROBERTO FIRMINO

Roberto Firmino is a box-to-box midfielder with great energy and a perfect passing technique over both long and short distances. He usually plays as a second attacker with a superb left foot, but also surprises defenders with his heading ability.

BIRTHDATE	02/10/1991
POSITION	ATT/STRIKER
HEIGHT	1.81 M
WEIGHT	76 KG
PREFERRED FOOT	RIGHT

ASSISTS
71

APPEARANCES
352

DRIBBLES
1454

PASSES
12419

SUCCESSFUL PASSES
76.3%

PENALTIES SCORED
5

GOALS
110

SHOTS
839

CHANCES CREATED
575

TACKLES
700

MAJOR CLUB HONOURS

- ⚽ Champions League: runner-up 2018, winner 2019
- ⚽ UEFA Europa League: runner-up 2016
- ⚽ UEFA Super Cup: 2019
- ⚽ FIFA Club World Cup: 2019

INTERNATIONAL HONOURS

- ⚽ Copa América: 2019

ACTIVITY AREAS

ANDRÉS GUARDADO

The hugely experienced Andrés Guardado is a creative player with excellent vision, whose game is based on winning the ball back with smart interceptions and then pushing forward either by dribbling or making a defence-splitting pass.

NATIONAL TEAM
Mexico

CURRENT CLUB
Real Betis

BIRTHDATE	28/09/1986
POSITION	ATTACKING
HEIGHT	1.69 M
WEIGHT	60 KG
PREFERRED FOOT	LEFT

ASSISTS
37

APPEARANCES
273

DRIBBLES
512

PENALTIES SCORED
6

PASSES
10195

SUCCESSFUL PASSES
84.0%

GOALS
16

SHOTS
327

CHANCES CREATED
323

TACKLES
333

MAJOR CLUB HONOURS
⚽ UEFA Intertoto Cup: 2008 (Deportivo)
⚽ Eredivisie: 2015, 2016 (PSV Eindhoven)

INTERNATIONAL HONOURS
⚽ CONCACAF Gold Cup: 2011, 2015, 2019
⚽ CONCACAF Cup: 2015

ACTIVITY AREAS

43

NATIONAL TEAM
Belgium

CURRENT CLUB
Real Madrid

EDEN HAZARD

Playing as an attacking midfielder or winger, Eden Hazard is one of the best at running with the ball and taking players on. He is known for his creativity, speed and technical ability, and is capable of changing the game with a turn of pace or dribble.

BIRTHDATE	07/01/1991
POSITION	SECOND STRIKER
HEIGHT	1.75 M
WEIGHT	74 KG
PREFERRED FOOT	BOTH

ASSISTS
105

APPEARANCES
482

DRIBBLES
2639

PENALTIES SCORED
31

PASSES
20132
SUCCESSFUL PASSES
83.4%

GOALS
135

SHOTS
874

CHANCES CREATED
1045

TACKLES
306

MAJOR CLUB HONOURS
- Ligue 1: 2011 (Lille)
- Premier League: 2015, 2017 (Chelsea)
- UEFA Europa League: 2013, 2019 (Chelsea)
- FIFA Club World Cup: runner up 2012 (Chelsea)

INTERNATIONAL HONOURS
- FIFA World Cup: third-place 2018

ACTIVITY AREAS

FRENKIE DE JONG

Frenkie de Jong has been an outstanding talent ever since he burst on to the scene as a teenager. His close control, accuracy, work rate, passing accuracy and movement have seen him being compared to the great Johan Cruyff.

NATIONAL TEAM
Netherlands

CURRENT CLUB
Barcelona

BIRTHDATE	12/05/1997
POSITION	CENTRAL
HEIGHT	1.80 M
WEIGHT	74 KG
PREFERRED FOOT	RIGHT

APPEARANCES
48

ASSISTS
2

DRIBBLES
95

PENALTIES SCORED
0

PASSES
2802
SUCCESSFUL PASSES
91.0%

GOALS
2

SHOTS
10

CHANCES CREATED
36

TACKLES
69

MAJOR CLUB HONOURS
- Eredivisie: 2019 (Ajax)
- KNVB Cup: 2019 (Ajax)
- UEFA Europa League: runner-up 2017 (Ajax)

INTERNATIONAL HONOURS
- UEFA Nations League: runner-up: 2019 (Ajax)

ACTIVITY AREAS

NATIONAL TEAM
France

CURRENT CLUB
Chelsea

N'GOLO KANTÉ

Defensive midfielder, N'Golo Kanté, has pace, boundless energy and great positional awareness. He frequently breaks up attacks with timely tackles, blocks and interceptions, then makes accurate passes. He has an eye for goal, too.

BIRTHDATE	29/03/1991
POSITION	CENTRAL
HEIGHT	1.68 M
WEIGHT	68 M
PREFERRED FOOT	RIGHT

ASSISTS
15

APPEARANCES
216

DRIBBLES
447

PENALTIES SCORED
0

PASSES
10961

SUCCESSFUL PASSES
85.8%

GOALS
12

SHOTS
162

CHANCES CREATED
219

TACKLES
750

MAJOR CLUB HONOURS
⚽ Premier League: 2016 (Leicester City) 2017
⚽ UEFA Europa League: 2019

INTERNATIONAL HONOURS
⚽ FIFA World Cup: 2018

ACTIVITY AREAS

BLAISE MATUIDI

Blaise Matuidi has everything a coach wants from a holding midfielder. He is a superb tackler, hard-working and an accurate passer who is able to go from box to box, breaking up attacks at one end and scoring at the other.

NATIONAL TEAM
France

CURRENT CLUB
Juventus

BIRTHDATE	09/04/1987
POSITION	CENTRAL
HEIGHT	1.80 M
WEIGHT	75 KG
PREFERRED FOOT	LEFT

ASSISTS
37

APPEARANCES
566

DRIBBLES
748

PENALTIES SCORED
0

PASSES
24147
SUCCESSFUL PASSES
88.0%

GOALS
44

SHOTS
399

CHANCES CREATED
392

TACKLES
1380

MAJOR CLUB HONOURS
⚽ Ligue 1: 2013, 2014, 2015, 2016 (Paris Saint-Germain)
⚽ Serie A: 2018, 2019

INTERNATIONAL HONOURS
⚽ FIFA World Cup: 2018

ACTIVITY AREAS

21

NATIONAL TEAM
Serbia

CURRENT CLUB
Lazio

SERGEJ MILINKOVIĆ-SAVIĆ

Effective in and around both penalty areas, Sergej Milinković-Savić is a top-class midfielder. He is blessed with great energy and sound technique, and is also good at stopping opposition attacks and launching his own team's raids.

BIRTHDATE	27/02/1995
POSITION	CENTRAL
HEIGHT	1.91 M
WEIGHT	76 KG
PREFERRED FOOT	RIGHT

APPEARANCES
174

ASSISTS
21

DRIBBLES
384

PASSES
7515
SUCCESSFUL PASSES
76.3%

PENALTIES SCORED
0

GOALS
31

SHOTS
359

CHANCES CREATED
226

TACKLES
282

MAJOR CLUB HONOURS
⚽ Coppa Italia: 2019

INTERNATIONAL HONOURS
⚽ UEFA European Under-19 Championship: 2013
⚽ FIFA U-20 World Cup: 2015

ACTIVITY AREAS

48

LUKA MODRIĆ

Playmaker Luka Modrić is often at the heart of his team's best attacking moves. He has a great footballing brain, can deliver long and short passes with both feet and strike powerful long-range shots, especially free-kicks.

NATIONAL TEAM
Croatia

CURRENT CLUB
Real Madrid

BIRTHDATE	09/09/1985
POSITION	ATTACKING
HEIGHT	1.72 M
WEIGHT	66 KG
PREFERRED FOOT	RIGHT

APPEARANCES
444

ASSISTS
59

DRIBBLES
1167

PASSES
24543

SUCCESSFUL PASSES
88.5%

PENALTIES SCORED
3

GOALS
37

SHOTS
559

CHANCES CREATED
715

TACKLES
648

MAJOR CLUB HONOURS
- ⚽ La Liga: 2017
- ⚽ UEFA Champions League: 2014, 2016, 2017, 2018
- ⚽ UEFA Super Cup: 2014, 2016, 2017
- ⚽ FIFA Club World Cup: 2014, 2016, 2017, 2018

INTERNATIONAL HONOURS
- ⚽ FIFA World Cup: runner-up 2018

ACTIVITY AREAS

25

 **NATIONAL TEAM**
Germany

CURRENT CLUB
Bayern Munich

THOMAS MÜLLER

Thomas Müller is a dangerous attacking midfielder, who scores countless goals playing just behind a lone striker. The German powerhouse is mentally strong, tactically clever and great at finding holes in the opposition's defence.

BIRTHDATE	13/09/1989
POSITION	SECOND STRIKER
HEIGHT	1.86 M
WEIGHT	75 KG
PREFERRED FOOT	RIGHT

APPEARANCES 454

ASSISTS 128

DRIBBLES 910

PASSES 14260

SUCCESSFUL PASSES 76.9%

PENALTIES SCORED 20

GOALS 160

SHOTS 943

CHANCES CREATED 813

TACKLES 476

MAJOR CLUB HONOURS
⚽ Bundesliga: x 8 between 2010 and 2019
⚽ UEFA Champions League: 2013
⚽ UEFA Super Cup: 2013
⚽ FIFA Club World Cup: 2013

INTERNATIONAL HONOURS
⚽ FIFA World Cup: 2014

ACTIVITY AREAS

MIRALEM PJANIĆ

An old-fashioned playmaker, Miralem Pjanić is great on the ball and can spray passes all around the pitch. His right-foot is like a magic wand at free-kicks, curling or driving shots past the wall and he creates chances for team-mates, too.

NATIONAL TEAM
Bosnia & Herzegovina

CURRENT CLUB
Juventus

BIRTHDATE	02/04/1990
POSITION	CENTRAL
HEIGHT	1.80 M
WEIGHT	72 KG
PREFERRED FOOT	BOTH

APPEARANCES
470

ASSISTS
93

DRIBBLES
729

PENALTIES SCORED
7

PASSES
24163

SUCCESSFUL PASSES
86.6%

GOALS
66

SHOTS
756

CHANCES CREATED
884

TACKLES
661

MAJOR CLUB HONOURS
⚽ Serie A: 2017, 2018, 2019
⚽ Coppa Italia: 2017, 2018

INTERNATIONAL HONOURS
⚽ None to date

ACTIVITY AREAS

NATIONAL TEAM
France

CURRENT CLUB
Manchester United

PAUL POGBA

Known for his strength, speed and athleticism, Paul Pogba glides across the pitch on and off the ball, stopping attacks at one end before finishing off his team's rapid counter-attack. Good with both feet, Pogba is lethal in front of goal.

BIRTHDATE	15/03/1993
POSITION	CENTRAL
HEIGHT	1.91 M
WEIGHT	84 KG
PREFERRED FOOT	RIGHT

APPEARANCES
296

ASSISTS
57

DRIBBLES
1105

PASSES
15177

PENALTIES SCORED
10

SUCCESSFUL PASSES
83.6%

GOALS
60

SHOTS
740

CHANCES CREATED
411

TACKLES
560

MAJOR CLUB HONOURS
- ⚽ Serie A: x 4 between 2013 and 2016 (Juventus)
- ⚽ UEFA Europa League: 2017

INTERNATIONAL HONOURS
- ⚽ FIFA World Cup: 2018

ACTIVITY AREAS

RENATO SANCHES

Renato Sanches can play in almost every midfield position: defensive, wide, central or as a creative playmaker. Calm in possession, he is a fine passer, strong tackler and isn't afraid of shooting from distance.

 NATIONAL TEAM
Portugal

CURRENT CLUB
Lille

BIRTHDATE	18/08/1997
POSITION	CENTRAL
HEIGHT	1.76 M
WEIGHT	70 KG
PREFERRED FOOT	RIGHT

APPEARANCES
89

ASSISTS
2

DRIBBLES
250

PASSES
2725

SUCCESSFUL PASSES
86.3%

PENALTIES SCORED
0

GOALS
5

SHOTS
84

CHANCES CREATED
65

TACKLES
72

MAJOR CLUB HONOURS
⚽ Bundesliga: 2017, 2019

INTERNATIONAL HONOURS
⚽ UEFA European Championship: 2016

ACTIVITY AREAS

53

7

NATIONAL TEAM
Korea Republic

CURRENT CLUB
Tottenham Hotspur

SON HEUNG-MIN

Son Heung-Min is at his best when he plays behind the main striker. Although excellent with both feet, attacking from the right side is his strength and he converts a lot of chances that are set up by knock-downs or passes across the box.

BIRTHDATE	08/07/1992
POSITION	WINGER
HEIGHT	1.83 M
WEIGHT	78 KG
PREFERRED FOOT	BOTH

ASSISTS
42

APPEARANCES
342

DRIBBLES
1098

PENALTIES SCORED
0

PASSES
7683

SUCCESSFUL PASSES
81.2%

GOALS
112

SHOTS
752

CHANCES CREATED
336

TACKLES
294

MAJOR CLUB HONOURS
⚽ UEFA Champions League: runner-up 2019

INTERNATIONAL HONOURS
⚽ AFC Asian Cup: runner-up 2015

ACTIVITY AREAS

MARCO VERRATTI

Marco Verrati is an awesome ball-playing midfielder. He is able to dribble past defenders at speed to set up chances for the players ahead of him. He can pass or shoot accurately and powerfully with both feet.

NATIONAL TEAM
Italy

CURRENT CLUB
Paris Saint-Germain

6

BIRTHDATE	05/11/1992
POSITION	CENTRAL
HEIGHT	1.65 M
WEIGHT	60 KG
PREFERRED FOOT	RIGHT

APPEARANCES
520

ASSISTS
80

DRIBBLES
954

PENALTIES SCORED
0

PASSES
42724
SUCCESSFUL PASSES
91.1%

GOALS
16

SHOTS
144

CHANCES CREATED
570

TACKLES
1462

MAJOR CLUB HONOURS
⚽ Ligue 1: x 6 (between 2013 and 2019)
⚽ Coupe de France: x 4 (between 2015 and 2018)

INTERNATIONAL HONOURS
⚽ UEFA European U-21 Championship: runner-up 2013

ACTIVITY AREAS

5

CURRENT CLUB
Liverpool

GEORGINIO WIJNALDUM

Georginio Wijnaldum can play anywhere in the middle of the pitch as an attacking playmaker or a defensive shield for the back-line. Good with both feet and a strong tackler, he goes box to box and scores crucial goals, especially with headers.

BIRTHDATE	11/11/1990
POSITION	ATTACKING
HEIGHT	1.75 M
WEIGHT	69 KG
PREFERRED FOOT	RIGHT

APPEARANCES
229

ASSISTS
18

DRIBBLES
453

PASSES
9226
SUCCESSFUL
PASSES
88.2%

PENALTIES
SCORED
2

GOALS
36

SHOTS
284

CHANCES
CREATED
196

TACKLES
249

MAJOR CLUB HONOURS
- ⚽ UEFA Champions League: 2019, runner-up 2018
- ⚽ UEFA Super Cup: 2019
- ⚽ FIFA Club World Cup: 2019

INTERNATIONAL HONOURS
- ⚽ UEFA Nations League: runner-up: 2019
- ⚽ FIFA World Cup: third place 2014

ACTIVITY AREAS

AXEL WITSEL

Originally a pacy right-winger, Axel Witsel has developed into a strong central midfielder for his club. He frequently drives his team forward with both his play and leadership skills. He is especially good at delivering dangerous passes with either foot.

 **NATIONAL TEAM**
Belgium

CURRENT CLUB
Borussia Dortmund

BIRTHDATE	12/01/1989
POSITION	CENTRAL
HEIGHT	1.86 M
WEIGHT	81 KG
PREFERRED FOOT	RIGHT

ASSISTS
9

APPEARANCES
141

DRIBBLES
180

PENALTIES SCORED
1

PASSES
8193
SUCCESSFUL PASSES
90.7%

GOALS
17

SHOTS
161

CHANCES CREATED
89

TACKLES
258

MAJOR CLUB HONOURS
⚽ DFL-Supercup: 2019

INTERNATIONAL HONOURS
⚽ FIFA World Cup: third place 2018

ACTIVITY AREAS

FORWARDS

The forwards, or strikers, are a team's frontline attackers and the chief goalscorers. They are also the team's most celebrated players. Whether it is the smaller, quicker player, such as Lionel Messi and Sergio Agüero, or the bigger, more physical attacker, such as Cristiano Ronaldo and Romelu Lukaku, strikers have perfected the ability to find the back of the net on a regular basis. Aside from scoring lots of goals the world's best strikers are also effective in creating chances for team-mates.

WHAT DO THE STATS MEAN?

GOALS

This is the total number of goals a striker has scored. The figure spans across all the top clubs the player has represented so far in their career.

75%

CONVERSION RATE

The percentage shows how good the player is at taking their chance in front of goal – if a player scores two goals from four shots, their conversion rate is 50%.

ASSISTS

A pass, cross or header to a team-mate who then scores counts as an assist. This stat also includes a deflected shot that is immediately converted by a team-mate.

128

MINUTES PER GOAL

This is the average length of time it takes for the player to score. It is calculated across all the minutes the player has played in their career at top level.

Did you know?

In Germany, the definition of a hat-trick is when a player scores three goals in the same half. The goals must also come in a row, without another player from the same team or the opposition scoring in between.

NATIONAL TEAM
Argentina

CURRENT CLUB
Manchester City

SERGIO AGÜERO

Sergio Agüero is one of the most complete strikers in world football today. Good coming in from either wing or down the centre, he can beat defenders on the dribble or with his pace, then shoot powerfully and accurately with either foot.

BIRTHDATE	02/06/1988
POSITION	STRIKER
HEIGHT	1.73 M
WEIGHT	70 KG
PREFERRED FOOT	RIGHT

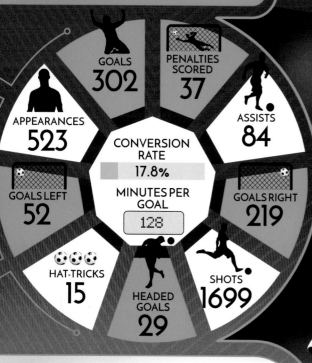

GOALS
302

PENALTIES SCORED
37

ASSISTS
84

APPEARANCES
523

CONVERSION RATE
17.8%

MINUTES PER GOAL
128

GOALS LEFT
52

GOALS RIGHT
219

HAT-TRICKS
15

HEADED GOALS
29

SHOTS
1699

MAJOR CLUB HONOURS
⚽ UEFA Europa League: 2010 (Atlético Madrid) ⚽ UEFA Super Cup: 2010 (Atlético Madrid) ⚽ Premier League: 2012, 2014, 2018, 2019 ⚽ FA Cup: 2019

INTERNATIONAL HONOURS
⚽ Olympic Games: gold medal 2008
⚽ FIFA World Cup: runner-up 2014
⚽ Copa América: runner-up 2015, 2016

ACTIVITY AREAS

PIERRE-EMERICK AUBAMEYANG

Pierre-Emerick Aubameyang not only leads the line as a striker, but he is a great team leader as captain. He often beats the opposition defence with his speed and off-the-ball movement, and is lethal in front of goal.

NATIONAL TEAM
Gabon

CURRENT CLUB
Arsenal

BIRTHDATE	18/06/1989
POSITION	STRIKER
HEIGHT	1.87 M
WEIGHT	80 KG
PREFERRED FOOT	RIGHT

GOALS
222

PENALTIES SCORED
17

APPEARANCES
406

ASSISTS
53

CONVERSION RATE
18.8%

MINUTES PER GOAL
141

GOALS LEFT
39

GOALS RIGHT
158

HAT-TRICKS
8

HEADED GOALS
24

SHOTS
1178

MAJOR CLUB HONOURS
- DFB-Pokal: 2017 (Borussia Dortmund)
- UEFA Europa League: runner-up 2019

INTERNATIONAL HONOURS
- King's Cup: third place 2018

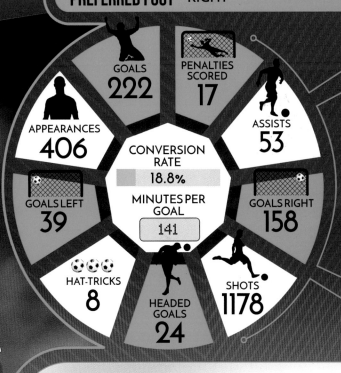

ACTIVITY AREAS

NATIONAL TEAM
Uruguay

CURRENT CLUB
Paris Saint-Germain

EDINSON CAVANI

Edinson Cavani is a fine dribbler, great at running into space and scoring spectacular goals, especially with overhead kicks. He has an impressive work rate, too, always hassling the opposition's defence to win the ball.

BIRTHDATE	14/02/1987
POSITION	STRIKER
HEIGHT	1.84 M
WEIGHT	71 KG
PREFERRED FOOT	RIGHT

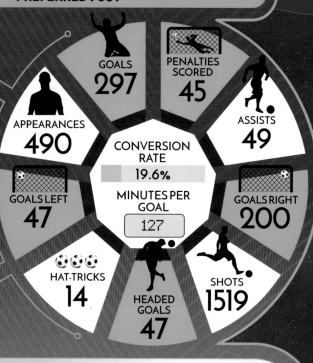

GOALS
297

PENALTIES SCORED
45

ASSISTS
49

APPEARANCES
490

CONVERSION RATE
19.6%

GOALS LEFT
47

MINUTES PER GOAL
127

GOALS RIGHT
200

HAT-TRICKS
14

HEADED GOALS
47

SHOTS
1519

MAJOR CLUB HONOURS
- Coppa Italia: 2012 (Napoli)
- Ligue 1: 2014, 2015, 2016, 2018, 2019
- Coupe de France: 2015, 2016, 2018, 2019

INTERNATIONAL HONOURS
- Copa América: 2019

ACTIVITY AREAS

62

MOUSSA DEMBÉLÉ

Moussa Dembélé has been playing top-division football since the age of 17. He is a tall, athletic and brave central striker who is amazingly quick to react when a chance presents itself. He is also very good in the air.

NATIONAL TEAM
France

CURRENT CLUB
Lyon

BIRTHDATE	12/07/1996
POSITION	STRIKER
HEIGHT	1.83 M
WEIGHT	73 KG
PREFERRED FOOT	RIGHT

GOALS 36

PENALTIES SCORED 6

ASSISTS 6

APPEARANCES 87

CONVERSION RATE 18.8%

MINUTES PER GOAL 169

GOALS LEFT 5

GOALS RIGHT 24

HAT-TRICKS 0

HEADED GOALS 5

SHOTS 192

MAJOR CLUB HONOURS
- Scottish Premiership: 2017, 2018 (Celtic)
- Scottish Cup: 2017, 2018 (Celtic)

INTERNATIONAL HONOURS
- None to date

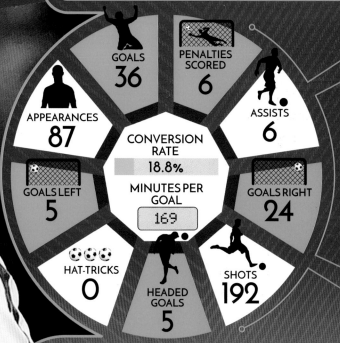

ACTIVITY AREAS

NATIONAL TEAM
Portugal

CURRENT CLUB
Atlético Madrid

JOÃO FÉLIX

João Félix is a talented attacker, who is showing great promise early in his career. He uses his superb balance and speed to run past defenders and set up goals, or arrive late in the penalty area to score with a powerful right-footed strike.

BIRTHDATE	10/11/1999
POSITION	FORWARD
HEIGHT	1.81 M
WEIGHT	70 KG
PREFERRED FOOT	RIGHT

GOALS
9

PENALTIES SCORED
2

ASSISTS
3

APPEARANCES
32

CONVERSION RATE
10.8%

MINUTES PER GOAL
264

GOALS LEFT
3

GOALS RIGHT
6

HAT-TRICKS
1

HEADED GOALS
0

SHOTS
83

MAJOR CLUB HONOURS
⚽ Primeira Liga: 2019 (Benfica)

INTERNATIONAL HONOURS
⚽ UEFA Nations League: 2019

ACTIVITY AREAS

ANTOINE GRIEZMANN

A brilliant forward who can score with either foot, Antoine Griezmann is a gifted footballer who can also cross, dribble, hold the ball and take players on. He is very active on the field, always looking for the ball and trying to beat the defence.

NATIONAL TEAM
France

CURRENT CLUB
Barcelona

BIRTHDATE	21/03/1991
POSITION	STRIKER
HEIGHT	1.76 M
WEIGHT	73 KG
PREFERRED FOOT	LEFT

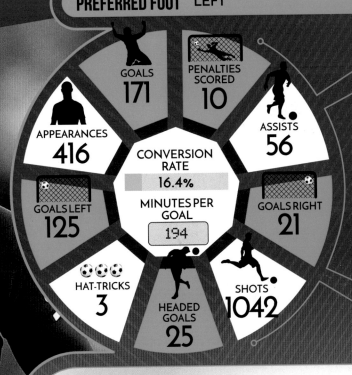

GOALS
171

PENALTIES SCORED
10

ASSISTS
56

APPEARANCES
416

CONVERSION RATE
16.4%

MINUTES PER GOAL
194

GOALS LEFT
125

GOALS RIGHT
21

HAT-TRICKS
3

HEADED GOALS
25

SHOTS
1042

MAJOR CLUB HONOURS
- UEFA Europa League: 2018 (Atlético Madrid)
- UEFA Super Cup: 2018 (Atlético Madrid)

INTERNATIONAL HONOURS
- FIFA World Cup: 2018

ACTIVITY AREAS

21

NATIONAL TEAM
Argentina

CURRENT CLUB
Juventus

GONZALO HIGUAÍN

Gonzalo Higuaín is capable of scoring great goals with either foot and can even out-jump taller defenders to win headers. He leads the line with power, speed and superb ball control, which makes him very difficult to defend against.

BIRTHDATE	10/12/1987
POSITION	STRIKER
HEIGHT	1.86 M
WEIGHT	89 KG
PREFERRED FOOT	RIGHT

GOALS
270

PENALTIES SCORED
19

APPEARANCES
530

ASSISTS
85

CONVERSION RATE
18.2%

MINUTES PER GOAL
137

GOALS LEFT
65

GOALS RIGHT
184

HAT-TRICKS
10

HEADED GOALS
19

SHOTS
1485

MAJOR CLUB HONOURS
⚽ UEFA Europa League: 2019 (Chelsea) ⚽ La Liga: 2007, 2008, 2012 (Real Madrid) ⚽ Coppa Italia: 2014 (Napoli), 2017, 2018 ⚽ Serie A: 2016, 2018

INTERNATIONAL HONOURS
⚽ FIFA World Cup: runner-up 2014
⚽ Copa América: runner-up 2015, 2016

ACTIVITY AREAS

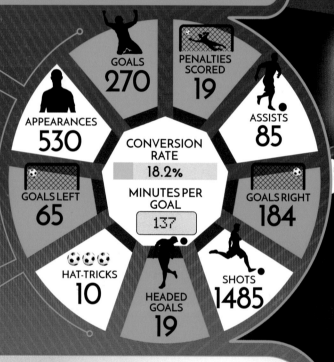

CIRO IMMOBILE

A great team-player, Ciro Immobile is a natural finisher who is excellent in the air. His goals tally is even higher because he refuses to give up lost causes and is willing to chase back to force mistakes out of defenders.

NATIONAL TEAM
Italy

CURRENT CLUB
Lazio

BIRTHDATE	20/02/1990
POSITION	STRIKER
HEIGHT	1.85 M
WEIGHT	78 KG
PREFERRED FOOT	RIGHT

GOALS
146

PENALTIES SCORED
30

APPEARANCES
274

ASSISTS
38

CONVERSION RATE
18.5%

GOALS LEFT
17

GOALS RIGHT
115

MINUTES PER GOAL
133

HAT-TRICKS
5

HEADED GOALS
14

SHOTS
790

MAJOR CLUB HONOURS
⚽ Coppa Italia: 2019 (Lazio)

INTERNATIONAL HONOURS
⚽ UEFA European U-21 Championship: runner-up 2013

ACTIVITY AREAS

18

NATIONAL TEAM
Serbia

CURRENT CLUB
Real Madrid

LUKA JOVIĆ

Luka Jović is a predator in the penalty box. He uses his speed and attacking instincts to find spaces in the penalty area and score goals from close range with deft touches from either foot and, occasionally, his head.

BIRTHDATE	23/12/1997
POSITION	STRIKER
HEIGHT	1.82 M
WEIGHT	85 KG
PREFERRED FOOT	RIGHT

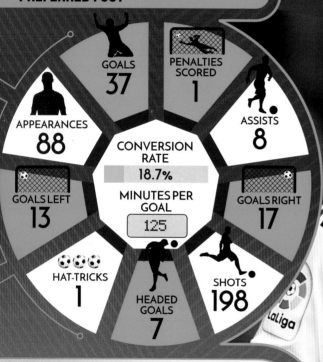

GOALS
37

PENALTIES SCORED
1

APPEARANCES
88

ASSISTS
8

CONVERSION RATE
18.7%

GOALS LEFT
13

MINUTES PER GOAL
125

GOALS RIGHT
17

HAT-TRICKS
1

HEADED GOALS
7

SHOTS
198

MAJOR CLUB HONOURS
⚽ Serbian SuperLiga: 2014 (Red Star Belgrade)
⚽ DFB-Pokal: 2018 (Eintracht Frankfurt)

INTERNATIONAL HONOURS
⚽ None to date

ACTIVITY AREAS

HARRY KANE

A natural striker, Harry Kane is known for scoring goals from long- or short-range, with his head or either foot. His pace, shooting accuracy and aerial strength have made him prolific for both club and country in recent years.

NATIONAL TEAM
England

CURRENT CLUB
Tottenham Hotspur

BIRTHDATE	28/07/1993
POSITION	STRIKER
HEIGHT	1.88 M
WEIGHT	86 KG
PREFERRED FOOT	RIGHT

GOALS
164

PENALTIES SCORED
23

ASSISTS
26

APPEARANCES
251

CONVERSION RATE
18.1%

MINUTES PER GOAL
121

GOALS LEFT
37

GOALS RIGHT
98

HAT-TRICKS
10

HEADED GOALS
28

SHOTS
908

MAJOR CLUB HONOURS
⚽ UEFA Champions League: runner-up 2019

INTERNATIONAL HONOURS
⚽ UEFA Nations League: third place 2019

ACTIVITY AREAS

9

ROBERT LEWANDOWSKI

Robert Lewandowski has consistently ranked as one of the world's best strikers ever since he made his debut at Borussia Dortmund in 2010. His positioning, technique, power and finishing have seen him net more than 150 goals for Bayern.

BIRTHDATE	21/08/1988
POSITION	STRIKER
HEIGHT	1.84 M
WEIGHT	80 KG
PREFERRED FOOT	RIGHT

GOALS 292

PENALTIES SCORED 35

ASSISTS 58

APPEARANCES 405

CONVERSION RATE 19.1%

MINUTES PER GOAL 111

GOALS LEFT 49

GOALS RIGHT 194

HAT-TRICKS 12

HEADED GOALS 46

SHOTS 1529

MAJOR CLUB HONOURS
⚽ UEFA Champions League: runner-up 2013 (Borussia Dortmund) ⚽ Bundesliga: 2011, 2012 (Borussia Dortmund), 2015, 2016, 2017, 2018, 2019 ⚽ DFB-Pokal: 2012 (Borussia Dortmund), 2016, 2019

INTERNATIONAL HONOURS
⚽ None to date

ACTIVITY AREAS

9

ROMELU LUKAKU

Romelu Lukaku often uses his size and strength to dispossess defenders before controlling the ball and unleashing a fierce shot or a pass to well-placed team-mate. He is also superb in the air and scores many headers.

NATIONAL TEAM
Belgium

CURRENT CLUB
Inter Milan

BIRTHDATE	13/05/1993
POSITION	STRIKER
HEIGHT	1.90 M
WEIGHT	94 KG
PREFERRED FOOT	LEFT

GOALS **154**

PENALTIES SCORED **13**

ASSISTS **45**

APPEARANCES **328**

CONVERSION RATE **17.7%**

MINUTES PER GOAL **161**

GOALS LEFT **81**

GOALS RIGHT **38**

HAT-TRICKS **4**

HEADED GOALS **33**

SHOTS **870**

MAJOR CLUB HONOURS
⚽ Belgian Pro League: 2010 (Anderlecht)

INTERNATIONAL HONOURS
⚽ FIFA World Cup: third place 2018

ACTIVITY AREAS

71

10

NATIONAL TEAM
Senegal

CURRENT CLUB
Liverpool

SADIO MANÉ

Sadio Mané has breathtaking pace and dribbling ability. Although he normally plays on the wing, he can also be dangerous in the middle of the park as he can leap high to win headers and shoot powerfully with either foot.

BIRTHDATE	10/04/1992
POSITION	FORWARD
HEIGHT	1.75 M
WEIGHT	69 KG
PREFERRED FOOT	RIGHT

GOALS
100

PENALTIES SCORED
0

APPEARANCES
226

ASSISTS
35

CONVERSION RATE
19.5%

MINUTES PER GOAL
178

GOALS LEFT
26

GOALS RIGHT
61

HAT-TRICKS
3

HEADED GOALS
13

SHOTS
512

MAJOR CLUB HONOURS
⚽ UEFA Champions League: 2019, runner-up 2018
⚽ UEFA Super Cup: 2019
⚽ FIFA Club World Cup: 2019

INTERNATIONAL HONOURS
⚽ CAF Africa Cup of Nations: runner-up 2019

ACTIVITY AREAS

KYLIAN MBAPPÉ

A FIFA World Cup winner with France at just 18, Kylian Mbappé may well be the best young striker in world football at the moment. He is a superb ball-player who consistently gets on the score sheet and sets up chances for team-mates.

NATIONAL TEAM
France

CURRENT CLUB
Paris Saint-Germain

BIRTHDATE	20/12/1998
POSITION	STRIKER
HEIGHT	1.78 M
WEIGHT	73 KG
PREFERRED FOOT	RIGHT

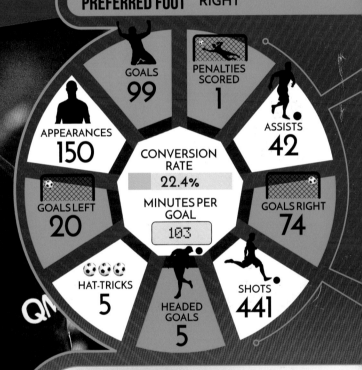

GOALS
99

PENALTIES SCORED
1

APPEARANCES
150

ASSISTS
42

CONVERSION RATE
22.4%

GOALS LEFT
20

MINUTES PER GOAL
103

GOALS RIGHT
74

HAT-TRICKS
5

HEADED GOALS
5

SHOTS
441

MAJOR CLUB HONOURS
⚽ Ligue 1: 2017 (Monaco), 2018, 2019, 2020
⚽ Coupe de France: 2018

INTERNATIONAL HONOURS
⚽ FIFA World Cup: 2018

ACTIVITY AREAS

10

NATIONAL TEAM
Argentina

CURRENT CLUB
Barcelona

LIONEL MESSI

The greatest player of his generation, if not the greatest ever, Lionel Messi is a fine playmaker with a stunning goal-scoring record. He is also a fantastically fast dribbler who can carve out opportunities to shoot with either foot, from any range.

BIRTHDATE	24/06/1987
POSITION	FORWARD
HEIGHT	1.70 M
WEIGHT	72 KG
PREFERRED FOOT	LEFT

GOALS
552

PENALTIES SCORED
67

ASSISTS
207

APPEARANCES
615

CONVERSION RATE
20.2%

MINUTES PER GOAL
90

GOALS LEFT
453

GOALS RIGHT
80

HAT-TRICKS
44

HEADED GOALS
18

SHOTS
2738

MAJOR CLUB HONOURS
⚽ UEFA Champions League: 2006, 2009, 2011, 2015 ⚽ UEFA Super Cup: 2009, 2011, 2015 ⚽ FIFA Club World Cup: 2009, 2011, 2015 ⚽ La Liga: 2005, 2006, 2009 2010, 2011, 2013, 2015, 2016, 2018, 2019

INTERNATIONAL HONOURS
⚽ FIFA World Cup: runner-up 2014
⚽ Olympic Games: gold medal 2008
⚽ Copa América: runner-up 2015, 2016

ACTIVITY AREAS

ÁLVARO MORATA

Álvaro Morata is perfectly built for a central striker. Tall, strong and excellent in the air, he is comfortable with the ball at his feet. Morata is also surprisingly fast and has great tactical and positional awareness.

NATIONAL TEAM
Spain

CURRENT CLUB
Atlético Madrid*

*On loan from Chelsea

BIRTHDATE	23/10/1992
POSITION	STRIKER
HEIGHT	1.90 M
WEIGHT	84 KG
PREFERRED FOOT	RIGHT

GOALS 87

PENALTIES SCORED 2

ASSISTS 31

APPEARANCES 266

CONVERSION RATE 16.5%

MINUTES PER GOAL 157

GOALS LEFT 16

GOALS RIGHT 44

HAT-TRICKS 2

HEADED GOALS 27

SHOTS 526

MAJOR CLUB HONOURS
⚽ UEFA Champions League: 2014, 2017 (Real Madrid) ⚽
UEFA Super Cup: 2016 (Real Madrid) ⚽ FIFA Club World Cup:
2016 (Real Madrid) ⚽ La Liga: 2012, 2017 (Real Madrid) ⚽
Serie A: 2015, 2016 (Juventus)

INTERNATIONAL HONOURS
⚽ UEFA European U-21 Championship 2013

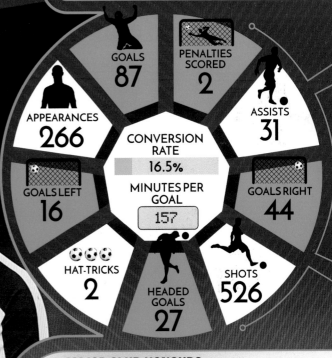

ACTIVITY AREAS

75

NATIONAL TEAM
Brazil

CURRENT CLUB
Paris Saint-Germain

NEYMAR JR

A natural-born flair player, Neymar Jr has a technique that is easy on the eye. He is great at beating defenders with his speed and trickery. More a No.10 than a No.9, he often scores from inside the six-yard box or outside the penalty area.

BIRTHDATE	05/02/1992
POSITION	STRIKER
HEIGHT	1.75 M
WEIGHT	68 KG
PREFERRED FOOT	RIGHT

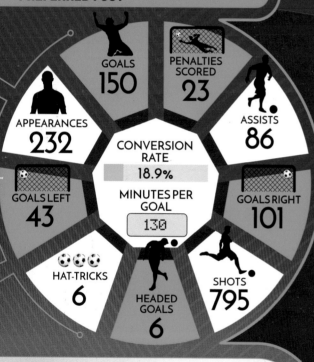

GOALS
150

PENALTIES SCORED
23

ASSISTS
86

APPEARANCES
232

CONVERSION RATE
18.9%

MINUTES PER GOAL
130

GOALS LEFT
43

GOALS RIGHT
101

HAT-TRICKS
6

HEADED GOALS
6

SHOTS
795

MAJOR CLUB HONOURS

⚽ Copa Libertadores: 2011 (Santos) ⚽ UEFA Champ League: 2016 (Barcelona) ⚽ FIFA Club World Cup: 2016 (Barcelona) ⚽ La Liga: 2015, 2016, 2017 (Barcelona) ⚽ Ligue 1: 2018, 2019, 2020 ⚽ Coupe de France: 2018

INTERNATIONAL HONOURS

⚽ FIFA Confederations Cup: 2013
⚽ Olympic Games: silver medal 2012, gold medal 2016

ACTIVITY AREAS

MARCO REUS

Marco Reus is an attacker who can lead the front line, play as a second striker or out wide. He is an expert finisher, especially with his right foot, and is also fantastic at setting up chances for his team-mates.

 **NATIONAL TEAM**
Germany

CURRENT CLUB
Borussia Dortmund

BIRTHDATE	31/05/1989
POSITION	FORWARD
HEIGHT	1.80 M
WEIGHT	71 KG
PREFERRED FOOT	RIGHT

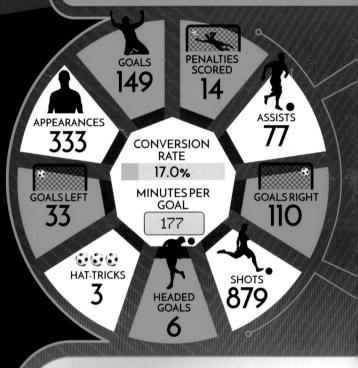

GOALS **149**

PENALTIES SCORED **14**

APPEARANCES **333**

ASSISTS **77**

CONVERSION RATE **17.0%**

MINUTES PER GOAL **177**

GOALS LEFT **33**

GOALS RIGHT **110**

HAT-TRICKS **3**

HEADED GOALS **6**

SHOTS **879**

MAJOR CLUB HONOURS
⚽ UEFA Champions League: runner-up 2013
⚽ DFB-Pokal: 2017

INTERNATIONAL HONOURS
⚽ None to date

ACTIVITY AREAS

NATIONAL TEAM
Portugal

CURRENT CLUB
Juventus

CRISTIANO RONALDO

The superstar striker has wowed fans across the world with his all-round attacking skills. He is breathtaking to watch when he is running at defences, brilliant in the air and a superb finisher, with an extraordinary goal-scoring record.

BIRTHDATE	05/02/1985
POSITION	FORWARD
HEIGHT	1.87 M
WEIGHT	83 KG
PREFERRED FOOT	RIGHT

GOALS **565**

PENALTIES SCORED **100**

APPEARANCES **710**

ASSISTS **170**

CONVERSION RATE **13.9%**

GOALS LEFT **95**

MINUTES PER GOAL **104**

GOALS RIGHT **375**

HAT-TRICKS **44**

HEADED GOALS **93**

SHOTS **4077**

MAJOR CLUB HONOURS

⚽ UEFA Champ League: 2008 (Man U), 2014, 2016, 2017, 2018 (R Mad) ⚽ FIFA Club World Cup: 2008 (Man U), 2014, 2016, 2017 (R Mad) ⚽ Prem League: 2007, 2008, 2009 (Man U) ⚽ La Liga: 2012, 2017 (R Mad) ⚽ Serie A: 2019

INTERNATIONAL HONOURS

⚽ UEFA European Championship: 2016
⚽ UEFA Nations League: 2019

ACTIVITY AREAS

78

MOHAMED SALAH

The two-time African Footballer of the Year is a brilliant left-footed attacker who prowls the left wing. Mo Salah has amazing pace with the ability to make angled runs, finding gaps in defences before scoring spectacular goals.

NATIONAL TEAM
Egypt

CURRENT CLUB
Liverpool

BIRTHDATE	15/06/1992
POSITION	FORWARD
HEIGHT	1.75 M
WEIGHT	71 KG
PREFERRED FOOT	LEFT

GOALS
134

PENALTIES SCORED
9

APPEARANCES
270

ASSISTS
58

CONVERSION RATE
16.6%

MINUTES PER GOAL
157

GOALS LEFT
106

GOALS RIGHT
24

HAT-TRICKS
3

HEADED GOALS
4

SHOTS
807

MAJOR CLUB HONOURS
- ⚽ UEFA Champions League: 2019, runner-up 2018
- ⚽ UEFA Super Cup: 2019
- ⚽ FIFA Club World Cup: 2019
- ⚽ Premier League: 2020

INTERNATIONAL HONOURS
- ⚽ CAF Africa Cup of Nations: runner-up 2017

ACTIVITY AREAS

7

RAHEEM STERLING

Raheem Sterling has become the complete forward at Manchester City. No longer a winger, he plays all over the front line, but is better behind a front man, coming off the left side and firing unstoppable shots with his preferred right foot.

BIRTHDATE	08/12/1994
POSITION	FORWARD
HEIGHT	1.70 M
WEIGHT	69 KG
PREFERRED FOOT	RIGHT

GOALS
96

PENALTIES SCORED
1

APPEARANCES
307

ASSISTS
55

CONVERSION RATE
15.5%

MINUTES PER GOAL
235

GOALS LEFT
27

GOALS RIGHT
65

HAT-TRICKS
4

HEADED GOALS
4

SHOTS
618

MAJOR CLUB HONOURS
⚽ Premier League: 2018, 2019
⚽ FA Cup: 2019

INTERNATIONAL HONOURS
⚽ UEFA Europa Nations League: third place 2019

ACTIVITY AREAS

LUIS SUÁREZ

Luis Suárez has a talent for scoring spectacular goals with his right foot, either facing or with his back to goal. He loves running at defenders and beating them with pace or dribbling trickery before smashing great shots past goalkeepers.

NATIONAL TEAM
Uruguay

CURRENT CLUB
Barcelona

BIRTHDATE	24/01/1987
POSITION	FORWARD
HEIGHT	1.82 M
WEIGHT	86 KG
PREFERRED FOOT	RIGHT

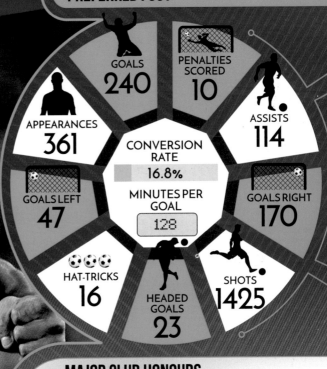

GOALS 240
PENALTIES SCORED 10
ASSISTS 114
APPEARANCES 361
CONVERSION RATE 16.8%
MINUTES PER GOAL 128
GOALS LEFT 47
GOALS RIGHT 170
HAT-TRICKS 16
HEADED GOALS 23
SHOTS 1425

MAJOR CLUB HONOURS

⚽ UEFA Champions League: 2015 ⚽ UEFA Super Cup: 2015 ⚽ FIFA Club World Cup: 2015 ⚽ La Liga: 2015, 2016, 2018, 2019 ⚽ Copa del Rey: 2015, 2016, 2017, 2018

INTERNATIONAL HONOURS

⚽ Copa América 2011

ACTIVITY AREAS

CURRENT CLUB
Leicester City

JAMIE VARDY

Jamie Vardy is an out-and-out No.9, leading the line and scoring goals. He has great pace and strength to beat defenders and shoot with either foot, though his right is better. Vardy is also brave and good in the air.

BIRTHDATE	11/01/1987
POSITION	STRIKER
HEIGHT	1.79 M
WEIGHT	74 KG
PREFERRED FOOT	RIGHT

GOALS 101

PENALTIES SCORED 18

APPEARANCES 211

ASSISTS 28

CONVERSION RATE 22.9%

MINUTES PER GOAL 170

GOALS LEFT 25

GOALS RIGHT 64

HAT-TRICKS 2

HEADED GOALS 12

SHOTS 441

MAJOR CLUB HONOURS
⚽ Premier League: 2016

INTERNATIONAL HONOURS
⚽ None to date

ACTIVITY AREAS

TIMO WERNER

Regarded as a complete goalscorer, Timo Werner uses his speed, strength and all-round skills to leave defenders trailing behind him before unleashing a powerful shot. He is equally good playing just behind the front man.

NATIONAL TEAM
Germany

CURRENT CLUB
RB Leipzig

BIRTHDATE	06/03/1996
POSITION	STRIKER
HEIGHT	1.80 M
WEIGHT	76 KG
PREFERRED FOOT	RIGHT

GOALS
95

PENALTIES SCORED
10

ASSISTS
39

APPEARANCES
233

CONVERSION RATE
16.8%

MINUTES PER GOAL
172

GOALS LEFT
14

GOALS RIGHT
70

HAT-TRICKS
2

HEADED GOALS
10

SHOTS
567

MAJOR CLUB HONOURS
⚽ None to date

INTERNATIONAL HONOURS
⚽ FIFA Confederations Cup: 2017

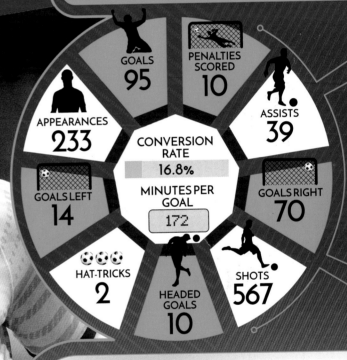

ACTIVITY AREAS

83

GOALKEEPERS

The goalkeeper is a team's last line of defence and unlike the other positions there is no one playing next to them. There is more pressure on goalkeepers than in any other position because when a keeper makes an error, the chances are that the other team will score. The goalies featured in this section are all great shot-stoppers, but some play outside their penalty areas as sweeper-keepers; others have made their reputation as penalty-savers; then there are the keepers who are great at catching the ball or punching it clear.

WHAT DO THE STATS MEAN?

CATCHES
This is the number of times the keeper has dealt with a dangerous ball – usually a cross – by catching the ball.

PENALTIES FACED/SAVED
This is the number of times a goalie has faced a penalty (excludes shoot-outs) and how successful they have been at saving it.

CLEAN SHEETS
Any occasion on which the goalie has not let in a goal for the full duration of the game counts as a clean sheet.

PUNCHES
This is a measure of how often the keeper has dealt with a dangerous ball (usually a cross) by punching it clear.

GOALS CONCEDED
This is the number of goals the keeper has conceded in their career in top-division football.

SAVES
This shows how many times the goalkeeper has stopped a shot or header that was on target.

Did you know?

In penalty shoot-outs, a goalkeeper statistically will save more by not diving. In practice, though, most goalkeepers try to predict the direction of the spot-kick and launch themselves with a dive!

1

NATIONAL TEAM
Brazil

CURRENT CLUB
Liverpool

ALISSON

The Brazilian has proved to be a top keeper at Liverpool. Alisson is a superb shot-stopper and great at dealing with crosses. Incredibly quick off his line to foil any threat, he can turn defence into attack by finding team-mates with long or short passes.

BIRTHDATE	02/10/1992
POSITION	GOALKEEPER
HEIGHT	1.91 M
WEIGHT	91 KG
PREFERRED FOOT	RIGHT

GOALS CONCEDED
109

APPEARANCES
135

PENALTIES SAVED
2

CLEAN SHEETS
63

SAVES
377

PENALTIES FACED
6

CATCHES
43

PUNCHES
46

MAJOR CLUB HONOURS
⚽ UEFA Champions League: 2019
⚽ FIFA Club World Cup: 2019

INTERNATIONAL HONOURS
⚽ Copa América: 2019

ACTIVITY AREAS

KEPA ARRIZABALAGA

Kepa Arrizabalaga is a confident keeper who delivers solid performances. Not only effective in open play, he is superb at saving penalties, especially in shoot-outs. Not a tall goalkeeper, he makes up for his size with his speed and agility.

NATIONAL TEAM
Spain

CURRENT CLUB
Chelsea

BIRTHDATE	03/10/1994
POSITION	GOALKEEPER
HEIGHT	1.86 M
WEIGHT	84 KG
PREFERRED FOOT	RIGHT

GOALS CONCEDED 153

APPEARANCES 133

PENALTIES SAVED 4

CLEAN SHEETS 42

SAVES 293

PENALTIES FACED 8

CATCHES 61

PUNCHES 42

MAJOR CLUB HONOURS
⚽ UEFA Europa League: 2019
⚽ EFL Cup: runner-up 2019

INTERNATIONAL HONOURS
⚽ UEFA European U-19 Championship: 2012

ACTIVITY AREAS

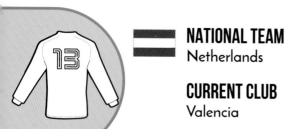

NATIONAL TEAM
Netherlands

CURRENT CLUB
Valencia

JASPER CILLESSEN

The Dutch keeper made appearances for giants Ajax and Barcelona before moving to Valencia. He is amazingly agile and can make great saves, be it high, low, to his right or left. He has excellent positional sense and works out his angles very well.

BIRTHDATE	22/04/1989
POSITION	GOALKEEPER
HEIGHT	1.85 M
WEIGHT	83 KG
PREFERRED FOOT	RIGHT

GOALS CONCEDED
66

APPEARANCES
54

PENALTIES SAVED
2

CLEAN SHEETS
13

SAVES
176

PENALTIES FACED
15

CATCHES
31

PUNCHES
31

MAJOR CLUB HONOURS
- ⚽ La Liga: 2018, 2019 (Barcelona)
- ⚽ Copa del Rey: 2017, 2018 (Barcelona)

INTERNATIONAL HONOURS
- ⚽ FIFA World Cup: third place 2014
- ⚽ UEFA Nations League: runner-up 2019

ACTIVITY AREAS

THIBAUT COURTOIS

Thibaut Courtois uses his height to dominate his penalty area, catching crosses and punching well. An agile shot-stopper, he can get down low to make saves, communicates well with his defence, is excellent coming off his line and passes well.

NATIONAL TEAM
Belgium

CURRENT CLUB
Real Madrid

BIRTHDATE	11/05/1992
POSITION	GOALKEEPER
HEIGHT	1.99 M
WEIGHT	96 KG
PREFERRED FOOT	LEFT

GOALS CONCEDED
323

APPEARANCES
341

PENALTIES SAVED
3

SAVES
805

CLEAN SHEETS
144

PENALTIES FACED
26

PUNCHES
118

CATCHES
407

MAJOR CLUB HONOURS
⚽ FIFA Club World Cup: 2018 ⚽ UEFA Europa League: 2012 (Atlético M) ⚽ UEFA Super Cup: 2012 (Atlético M) ⚽ La Liga: 2014 (Atlético M) ⚽ Premier League: 2015, 2017 (Chelsea)

INTERNATIONAL HONOURS
⚽ FIFA World Cup: third place 2018

ACTIVITY AREAS

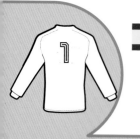

NATIONAL TEAM
Spain

CURRENT CLUB
Manchester United

DAVID DE GEA

David De Gea is an effective keeper, though unorthodox at times (he is known for using his legs to make saves). Agile and athletic, he marshals his penalty area well. His catching has improved, but he is still happier punching the ball the clear.

BIRTHDATE	07/11/1990
POSITION	GOALKEEPER
HEIGHT	1.92 M
WEIGHT	76 KG
PREFERRED FOOT	RIGHT

GOALS CONCEDED
462

APPEARANCES
427

PENALTIES SAVED
6

SAVES
1264

CLEAN SHEETS
143

PENALTIES FACED
41

PUNCHES
153

CATCHES
314

MAJOR CLUB HONOURS
⚽ UEFA Europa League: 2010 (Atlético Madrid), 2017
⚽ UEFA Super Cup: 2010 (Atlético Madrid)
⚽ Premier League: 2013 ⚽ FA Cup: 2016

INTERNATIONAL HONOURS
⚽ None to date

ACTIVITY AREAS

GIANLUIGI DONNARUMMA

The Italian is an amazing young talent who made his Serie A debut aged just 16 and won his first Italian cap at 17. Mentally strong and composed under pressure, he has everything it takes to become an all-time great.

NATIONAL TEAM
Italy

CURRENT CLUB
AC Milan

99

BIRTHDATE	25/02/1999
POSITION	GOALKEEPER
HEIGHT	1.96 M
WEIGHT	90 KG
PREFERRED FOOT	RIGHT

GOALS CONCEDED
186

APPEARANCES
174

PENALTIES SAVED
5

CLEAN SHEETS
57

SAVES
516

PENALTIES FACED
26

CATCHES
118

PUNCHES
98

MAJOR CLUB HONOURS
⚽ Supercoppa Italiana: 2016

INTERNATIONAL HONOURS
⚽ None to date

ACTIVITY AREAS

31

NATIONAL TEAM
Brazil

CURRENT CLUB
Manchester City

EDERSON

Owing to his range of passing and great ball skills, Ederson is often considered a playmaker goalkeeper and counted as one of the best in the English Premier League. He is a fine shot-stopper with a reputation for being a great penalty-kick saver, too.

BIRTHDATE	17/08/1993
POSITION	GOALKEEPER
HEIGHT	1.88 M
WEIGHT	86 KG
PREFERRED FOOT	LEFT

GOALS CONCEDED
116

APPEARANCES
136

PENALTIES SAVED
5

CLEAN SHEETS
57

SAVES
272

PENALTIES FACED
18

CATCHES
62

PUNCHES
41

MAJOR CLUB HONOURS
⚽ Premier League: 2018, 2019
⚽ FA Cup: 2019

INTERNATIONAL HONOURS
⚽ Copa América: 2019

ACTIVITY AREAS

92

EIJI KAWASHIMA

A goalkeeper who communicates well with his defenders, Eiji Kawashima's best asset is his ability to meet balls that seem way out of reach. His quick movement in the penalty area makes him good at anticipating and saving shots.

NATIONAL TEAM
Japan

CURRENT CLUB
Strasbourg

BIRTHDATE	20/03/1983
POSITION	GOALKEEPER
HEIGHT	1.85 M
WEIGHT	74 KG
PREFERRED FOOT	RIGHT

GOALS CONCEDED
76

APPEARANCES
41

PENALTIES SAVED
3

CLEAN SHEETS
5

SAVES
150

CATCHES
28

PENALTIES FACED
3

PUNCHES
13

MAJOR CLUB HONOURS
⚽ None to date

INTERNATIONAL HONOURS
⚽ AFC Asian Cup: 2011

ACTIVITY AREAS

NATIONAL TEAM
France

CURRENT CLUB
Tottenham Hotspur

HUGO LLORIS

Hugo Lloris is a natural leader, good at organising his defence. Armed with excellent reflexes, he is brilliant at coming off his line to clear the danger and then distributing the ball quickly, which has earned him the sweeper-keeper label.

BIRTHDATE	26/12/1986
POSITION	GOALKEEPER
HEIGHT	1.88 M
WEIGHT	82 KG
PREFERRED FOOT	LEFT

GOALS CONCEDED
582

APPEARANCES
552

PENALTIES SAVED
10

SAVES
1521

CLEAN SHEETS
188

PENALTIES FACED
58

PUNCHES
375

CATCHES
707

MAJOR CLUB HONOURS
⚽ UEFA Champions League: runner-up 2019
⚽ Coupe de France: 2012 (Olympique Lyonnais)

INTERNATIONAL HONOURS
⚽ FIFA World Cup: 2018

ACTIVITY AREAS

STEVE MANDANDA

After a brief stint in the Premier League, Steve Mandanda returned to Marseille, for whom he has made more than 500 appearances. His class and consistency have seen him win the Ligue 1 Goalkeeper of the Year award five times.

 **NATIONAL TEAM**
France

CURRENT CLUB
Marseille

BIRTHDATE	28/03/1985
POSITION	GOALKEEPER
HEIGHT	1.85 M
WEIGHT	82 KG
PREFERRED FOOT	RIGHT

GOALS CONCEDED
537

APPEARANCES
508

PENALTIES SAVED
12

CLEAN SHEETS
152

SAVES
1185

PENALTIES FACED
64

CATCHES
744

PUNCHES
196

MAJOR CLUB HONOURS
⚽ UEFA Europa League: runner-up 2018

INTERNATIONAL HONOURS
⚽ FIFA World Cup: 2018

ACTIVITY AREAS

NATIONAL TEAM
Costa Rica

CURRENT CLUB
Paris Saint-Germain

KEYLOR NAVAS

After fantastic performances at the 2014 FIFA World Cup, Keylor Navas earned a move to Europe and has since shown his quality and confidence at top-club level. He is an amazing shot-stopper, very agile, strong and great at dealing with crosses.

BIRTHDATE	15/12/1986
POSITION	GOALKEEPER
HEIGHT	1.85 M
WEIGHT	79 KG
PREFERRED FOOT	RIGHT

GOALS CONCEDED
214

APPEARANCES
228

PENALTIES SAVED
8

CLEAN SHEETS
88

SAVES
693

PENALTIES FACED
30

CATCHES
143

PUNCHES
97

MAJOR CLUB HONOURS
⚽ UEFA Champions League: 2016, 2017, 2018 (Real Madrid) ⚽ UEFA Super Cup: 2014, 2017 (Real Madrid) ⚽ FIFA Club World Cup: 2014, 2016, 2017, 2018 (Real Madrid) ⚽ La Liga: 2017 (Real Madrid)

INTERNATIONAL HONOURS
⚽ None to date

ACTIVITY AREAS

MANUEL NEUER

Manuel Neuer is famous for being football's first sweeper-keeper. He is a fine shot-stopper who commands his penalty area and marshals the defence well. He is also great with the ball at his feet, allowing defenders to play further upfield.

NATIONAL TEAM
Germany

CURRENT CLUB
Bayern Munich

BIRTHDATE	27/03/1986
POSITION	GOALKEEPER
HEIGHT	1.93 M
WEIGHT	92 KG
PREFERRED FOOT	RIGHT

GOALS CONCEDED
405

APPEARANCES
509

PENALTIES SAVED
10

CLEAN SHEETS
226

SAVES
1204

PENALTIES FACED
37

CATCHES
555

PUNCHES
241

MAJOR CLUB HONOURS
⚽ UEFA Champions League: 2013 ⚽ UEFA Super Cup: 2013 ⚽ FIFA Club World Cup: 2013 ⚽ Bundesliga: 2013, 2014, 2015, 2016, 2017, 2018, 2019 ⚽ DFB-Pokal: 2011 (Schalke 04), 2013, 2014, 2016, 2019

INTERNATIONAL HONOURS
⚽ FIFA World Cup: 2014

ACTIVITY AREAS

25

NATIONAL TEAM
Colombia

CURRENT CLUB
Napoli

DAVID OSPINA

David Ospina is considered to have very few weaknesses. He is excellent with crosses, equally happy punching or catching the ball and a super shot-stopper. What he lacks in height he makes up for with his agility and speed off his line.

BIRTHDATE	31/08/1988
POSITION	GOALKEEPER
HEIGHT	1.83 M
WEIGHT	80 KG
PREFERRED FOOT	RIGHT

GOALS CONCEDED
324

APPEARANCES
277

PENALTIES SAVED
6

CLEAN SHEETS
87

SAVES
841

PENALTIES FACED
32

CATCHES
428

PUNCHES
173

MAJOR CLUB HONOURS
⚽ FA Cup: 2015, 2017 (Arsenal)

INTERNATIONAL HONOURS
🌐 Copa América: third place 2016

ACTIVITY AREAS

98

JORDAN PICKFORD

Currently England's No1, Jordan Pickford is an agile and alert keeper who often starts moves from the back. He is also a big-match player and has won matches saving in shoot-outs and scoring in them, too.

NATIONAL TEAM
England

CURRENT CLUB
Everton

BIRTHDATE	07/03/1994
POSITION	GOALKEEPER
HEIGHT	1.85 M
WEIGHT	77 KG
PREFERRED FOOT	LEFT

GOALS CONCEDED
213

APPEARANCES
139

PENALTIES SAVED
4

CLEAN SHEETS
34

SAVES
447

PENALTIES FACED
16

CATCHES
95

PUNCHES
68

MAJOR CLUB HONOURS
⚽ None to date

INTERNATIONAL HONOURS
⚽ UEFA Nations League: third place 2019

ACTIVITY AREAS

NATIONAL TEAM
Denmark

CURRENT CLUB
Leicester City

KASPER SCHMEICHEL

Kasper Schmeichel, the son of the legendary keeper Peter Schmeichel, has many of his father's strengths. He is mentally strong and brilliant in one-on-one situations. He is also superb in the air, commands his penalty area and is a great ball distributor.

BIRTHDATE	05/11/1986
POSITION	GOALKEEPER
HEIGHT	1.89 M
WEIGHT	89 KG
PREFERRED FOOT	RIGHT

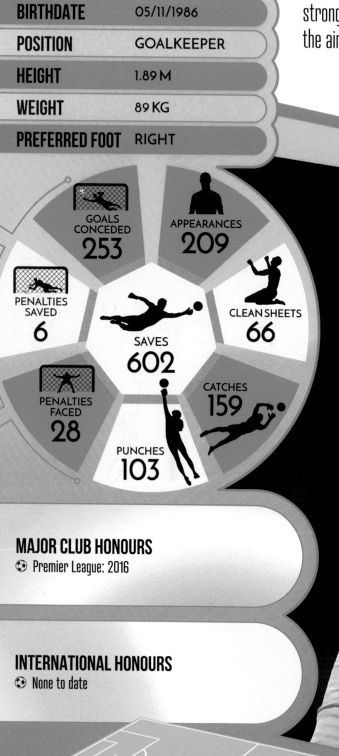

GOALS CONCEDED
253

APPEARANCES
209

PENALTIES SAVED
6

CLEAN SHEETS
66

SAVES
602

PENALTIES FACED
28

CATCHES
159

PUNCHES
103

MAJOR CLUB HONOURS
⚽ Premier League: 2016

INTERNATIONAL HONOURS
⚽ None to date

ACTIVITY AREAS

100

DANIJEL SUBAŠIĆ

Danijel Subašić is a formidable presence on the pitch. He is always well prepared and shows great mental strength, especially when he faces penalties. Dealing with crosses, Subašić has a strong arm and gets great distance when punching the ball clear.

NATIONAL TEAM
Croatia

CURRENT CLUB
Monaco

BIRTHDATE	27/10/1984
POSITION	GOALKEEPER
HEIGHT	1.91 M
WEIGHT	84 KG
PREFERRED FOOT	RIGHT

GOALS CONCEDED
234

APPEARANCES
227

PENALTIES SAVED
10

CLEAN SHEETS
85

SAVES
596

PENALTIES FACED
30

CATCHES
241

PUNCHES
75

MAJOR CLUB HONOURS
- ⚽ Ligue 1: 2017

INTERNATIONAL HONOURS
- ⚽ FIFA World Cup: runner-up 2018

ACTIVITY AREAS

1

NATIONAL TEAM
Poland

CURRENT CLUB
Juventus

WOJCIECH SZCZĘSNY

Wojciech Szczęsny has grown into one of Europe's top-class keepers. A natural shot-stopper with lightning reflexes, he is also great at controlling his penalty area, dealing with crosses and setting up counter-attacks with quick clearances.

BIRTHDATE	18/04/1990
POSITION	GOALKEEPER
HEIGHT	1.95 M
WEIGHT	90 KG
PREFERRED FOOT	RIGHT

GOALS CONCEDED
330

APPEARANCES
317

PENALTIES SAVED
10

CLEAN SHEETS
116

SAVES
863

PENALTIES FACED
49

CATCHES
311

PUNCHES
133

MAJOR CLUB HONOURS
- FA Cup: 2014, 2015 (Arsenal)
- Serie A: 2018, 2019
- Coppa Italia: 2018

INTERNATIONAL HONOURS
- None to date

ACTIVITY AREAS

MARC-ANDRÉ TER STEGEN

 **NATIONAL TEAM**
Germany

CURRENT CLUB
Barcelona

A brilliant sweeper-keeper, Marc-André ter Stegen is simply world class. In addition to his fine goalkeeping qualities, he is exceptional at anticipating opponents who have beaten the offside trap, and can rush off his line to meet the danger.

BIRTHDATE	30/04/1992
POSITION	GOALKEEPER
HEIGHT	1.87 M
WEIGHT	85 KG
PREFERRED FOOT	RIGHT

GOALS CONCEDED
307

APPEARANCES
314

PENALTIES SAVED
6

CLEAN SHEETS
123

SAVES
926

PENALTIES FACED
28

CATCHES
402

PUNCHES
145

MAJOR CLUB HONOURS
⚽ UEFA Champions League: 2015 ⚽ UEFA Super Cup: 2015 ⚽ FIFA Club World Cup: 2015 ⚽ La Liga: 2015, 2016, 2018, 2019 ⚽ Coppa del Rey: 2015, 2016, 2017, 2018

INTERNATIONAL HONOURS
⚽ FIFA Confederations Cup: 2017

ACTIVITY AREAS

MANAGERS

Coaches are as different to each other as players who play in different positions. But the majority of the 12 featured in this section have one thing in common: they are all winners, either in their domestic leagues or in continental competitions. Some, such as Zinedine Zidane, were legendary players in their own right and title winners well before they entered management, while others, such as Liverpool boss Jürgen Klopp, did little on the field but have had great success as the brains behind a top side.

WHAT DO THE STATS MEAN?

GAMES MANAGED

This is the number of matches the coach has been in charge of across their career in top-flight football.

TEAMS MANAGED

The number of clubs, including national sides, that the coach has managed during their career to date.

WINS

This is the number of games the coach has won, including one leg of a cup-tie, even if the tie was lost on aggregate or penalties.

TROPHIES

The trophy list features the domestic honours a coach has won across all the teams they have managed as well as any major European titles.

Did you know?

Retired manager Fabio Capello has won a major league championship in seven (or nine, counting the two revoked titles with Juventus) of his 16 seasons as a coach in Europe's top domestic leagues.

CARLO ANCELOTTI

A former international player, Carlo Ancelotti, uses different systems depending on the opposition and players available. His favourite formation is 4—4—2, sometimes in a diamond, other times with four midfielders in a line across the pitch.

NATIONALITY
Italian

CURRENT CLUB
Everton

DEBUT YEAR: 1995

FIRST CLUB: REGGIANA

CLUBS MANAGED	GAMES	LEAGUE TITLES
10	944	4

WINS	DRAW	LOSSES
557	216	171

CHAMPIONS LEAGUE TROPHIES	EUROPA LEAGUE TROPHIES	OTHER TROPHIES*
3	0	4

*Excludes Super Cups

MAJOR CLUB HONOURS

- ⚽ UEFA Champions League: 2003, 2007 (Milan), 2014 (Real Madrid)
- ⚽ FIFA Club World Cup: 2003, 2007 (Milan), 2014 (Real Madrid)
- ⚽ UEFA Super Cup: 2007, 2014 (Real Madrid)
- ⚽ UEFA Intertoto Cup: 1999 (Juventus)
- ⚽ Serie A: 2004 (Milan)
- ⚽ Coppa Italia: 2003 (Milan)
- ⚽ Premier League: 2010 (Chelsea)
- ⚽ FA Cup: 2010 (Chelsea)
- ⚽ Ligue 1: 2013 (Paris St Germain)
- ⚽ Copa del Rey: 2014 (Real Madrid)
- ⚽ Bundesliga: 2017 (Bayern Munich)

ANTONIO CONTE

Although Antonio Conte varies his tactics and formations, they are always based on a strong defence, so his teams tend to be great counter-attackers. Always animated on the touchline, he instils a great team spirit into his side.

NATIONALITY
Italian

CURRENT CLUB
Inter Milan

DEBUT YEAR: 2006

FIRST CLUB: AREZZO

CLUBS MANAGED	GAMES	LEAGUE TITLES
8	268	4

WINS	DRAW	LOSSES
171	56	41

CHAMPIONS LEAGUE TROPHIES	EUROPA LEAGUE TROPHIES	OTHER TROPHIES*
0	0	2

MAJOR CLUB HONOURS
- ⚽ Serie A: 2012, 2013, 2014 (Juventus)
- ⚽ Premier League: 2017 (Chelsea)
- ⚽ FA Cup: 2018 (Chelsea)

*Excludes Super Cups

PEP GUARDIOLA

Once a great midfielder himself, Pep Guardiola devised the *tika-taka* passing system at Barcelona (2008-12). Disciplined in possession, without the ball his teams press the opposition into making mistakes and then launch rapid counter-attacks.

NATIONALITY
Spanish

CURRENT CLUB
Manchester City

DEBUT YEAR: 2008

FIRST CLUB: BARCELONA

CLUBS MANAGED	GAMES	LEAGUE TITLES
3	517	8

WINS	DRAW	LOSSES
377	80	60

CHAMPIONS LEAGUE TROPHIES	EUROPA LEAGUE TROPHIES	OTHER TROPHIES*
2	0	8

MAJOR CLUB HONOURS

- ⚽ UEFA Champions League: 2009, 2011 (Barcelona)
- ⚽ UEFA Super Cup: 2009, 2011 (Barcelona), 2013 (Bayern Munich)
- ⚽ FIFA Club World Cup: 2009, 2011 (Barcelona), 2013 (Bayern Munich)
- ⚽ La Liga: 2009, 2010, 2011 (Barcelona)
- ⚽ Copa del Rey: 2009, 2012 (Barcelona)
- ⚽ Bundesliga: 2014, 2015, 2016 (Bayern Munich)
- ⚽ DFB-Pokal: 2014, 2016 (Bayern Munich)
- ⚽ Premier League: 2018, 2019
- ⚽ FA Cup: 2019

*Excludes Super Cups

JÜRGEN KLOPP

Jürgen Klopp brings great enthusiasm to the technical area and expects his team to show a similar spirit. His team are strong defensively, try to win back the ball immediately after they lose it and counter-attack at great speed.

NATIONALITY
German

CURRENT CLUB
Liverpool

DEBUT YEAR: 2001

FIRST CLUB: MAINZ 05

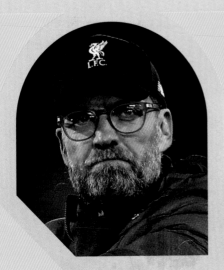

CLUBS MANAGED	GAMES	LEAGUE TITLES
3	607	2

WINS	DRAW	LOSSES
321	144	142

CHAMPIONS LEAGUE TROPHIES	EUROPA LEAGUE TROPHIES	OTHER TROPHIES*
1	0	1

MAJOR CLUB HONOURS

- ⚽ UEFA Champions League: runner-up 2013 (Borussia Dortmund), runner-up 2018, winner 2019
- ⚽ UEFA Super Cup: 2019
- ⚽ FIFA Club World Cup: 2019
- ⚽ Bundesliga: 2011, 2012 (Borussia Dortmund)
- ⚽ DFB-Pokal: 2012 (Borussia Dortmund)
- ⚽ Premier League: 2020

*Excludes Super Cups

JOSÉ MOURINHO

NATIONALITY
Portuguese

CURRENT CLUB
Tottenham Hotspur

José Mourinho focuses his team strength on midfield, normally with a player in front of the defence and two or three further upfield. He expects his defenders to be tactically and technically excellent, and tends to pick experienced players.

DEBUT YEAR:	2000
FIRST CLUB:	BENFICA

CLUBS MANAGED	GAMES	LEAGUE TITLES
8	692	8

WINS	DRAW	LOSSES
433	150	109

CHAMPIONS LEAGUE TROPHIES	EUROPA LEAGUE TROPHIES	OTHER TROPHIES*
2	2	8

MAJOR CLUB HONOURS
- ⚽ UEFA Champions League: 2004 (Porto), 2010 (Inter Milan)
- ⚽ UEFA Europa League: 2017 (Manchester United)
- ⚽ UEFA Cup: 2003 (Porto)
- ⚽ Premier League: 2005, 2006, 2015 (Chelsea)
- ⚽ FA Cup: 2006 (Chelsea)
- ⚽ Serie A: 2009, 2010 (Inter Milan)
- ⚽ Coppa Italia: 2010 (Inter Milan)
- ⚽ La Liga: 2012 (Real Madrid)
- ⚽ Copa del Rey: 2011 (Real Madrid)

*Excludes Super Cups

CLAUDE PUEL

NATIONALITY
French

CURRENT CLUB
Saint-Étienne

Claude Puel has managed at the highest levels in England and France for 20 years. He builds his teams from the back; they are always well organised and work very hard. Most teams he takes charge of show immediate improvements in their form.

DEBUT YEAR:	1999
FIRST CLUB:	MONACO

CLUBS MANAGED	GAMES	LEAGUE TITLES
7	776	1

WINS	DRAW	LOSSES
316	215	245

CHAMPIONS LEAGUE TROPHIES	EUROPA LEAGUE TROPHIES	OTHER TROPHIES*
0	0	1

MAJOR CLUB HONOURS
- ⚽ UEFA Intertoto Cup: 2004 (Lille)
- ⚽ Ligue 1: 2000 (Monaco)

*Excludes Super Cups

CLAUDIO RANIERI

NATIONALITY
Italian

CURRENT CLUB
Sampdoria

Claudio Ranieri relies on the 4—4—2 formation, with an emphasis on his team's defensive solidity, work-rate, fitness, pressing the opposition and then launching rapid counter-attacks. He is a great motivator and demands strong team spirit.

DEBUT YEAR:	1986
FIRST CLUB:	VIGOR LAMEZIA

CLUBS MANAGED	GAMES	LEAGUE TITLES
19	895	1

WINS	DRAW	LOSSES
406	248	241

CHAMPIONS LEAGUE TROPHIES	EUROPA LEAGUE TROPHIES	OTHER TROPHIES*
0	0	7

MAJOR CLUB HONOURS
- ⚽ UEFA Super Cup: 2004 (Valencia)
- ⚽ UEFA Intertoto Cup: 1998 (Valencia)
- ⚽ Coppa Italia: 1996 (Fiorentina)
- ⚽ Copa del Rey: 1999 (Valencia)
- ⚽ Premier League: 2016 (Leicester City)

*Excludes Super Cups

QUIQUE SETIÉN

NATIONALITY
Spanish

CURRENT CLUB
Barcelona

Quique Sétien, a former international player, has worked his way up the managerial ladder and is now recognised as a superb tactician. He wants his teams to be well organised, pass the ball quickly and work hard for each other.

DEBUT YEAR:	2001
FIRST CLUB:	R. SANTANDER

CLUBS MANAGED	GAMES	LEAGUE TITLES
7	161	0

WINS	DRAW	LOSSES
62	34	65

CHAMPIONS LEAGUE TROPHIES	EUROPA LEAGUE TROPHIES	OTHER TROPHIES*
0	0	0

MAJOR CLUB HONOURS
- ⚽ None to date

*Excludes Super Cups

DIEGO SIMEONE

Diego Simeone likes to use a formation which is almost a 4—2—2—2 unit, with wide midfielders playing between the two central ones and the strikers. Strong defensively, his teams are great defending set-pieces and dangerous in attack.

NATIONALITY
Argentinian

CURRENT CLUB
Atlético Madrid

DEBUT YEAR: 2006

FIRST CLUB: RACING CLUB

CLUBS MANAGED	GAMES	LEAGUE TITLES
7	429	1

WINS	DRAW	LOSSES
258	95	76

CHAMPIONS LEAGUE TROPHIES	EUROPA LEAGUE TROPHIES	OTHER TROPHIES*
0	2	3

*Excludes Super Cups

MAJOR CLUB HONOURS
- ⚽ UEFA Champions League: runner-up 2014, 2016
- ⚽ UEFA Europa League: 2012, 2018
- ⚽ UEFA Super Cup: 2012, 2018
- ⚽ La Liga: 2014
- ⚽ Copa del Rey: 2013

ANDRÉ VILLAS-BOAS

André Villas-Boas worked with former England coach Bobby Robson and José Mourinho before taking the main job himself. Most notably, he is the youngest-ever coach to win a major European trophy.

NATIONALITY
Portuguese

CURRENT CLUB
Marseille

DEBUT YEAR: 2009

FIRST CLUB: ACADÉMICA

CLUBS MANAGED	GAMES	LEAGUE TITLES
7	153	0

WINS	DRAW	LOSSES
87	37	29

CHAMPIONS LEAGUE TROPHIES	EUROPA LEAGUE TROPHIES	OTHER TROPHIES*
0	1	1

MAJOR CLUB HONOURS
- ⚽ UEFA Europa League: 2011 (Porto)

*Excludes Super Cups

DAVID WAGNER

David Wagner is showing great promise now that he has moved into top-flight football. He has achieved amazing results even against high-profile opponents. He is great at rallying his players when things are difficult.

NATIONALITY
German

CURRENT CLUB
Schalke 04

DEBUT YEAR: 2011

FIRST CLUB: B. DORTMUND II

CLUBS MANAGED	GAMES	LEAGUE TITLES
3	85	0

WINS	DRAW	LOSSES
20	25	40

CHAMPIONS LEAGUE TROPHIES	EUROPA LEAGUE TROPHIES	OTHER TROPHIES*
0	0	0

MAJOR CLUB HONOURS
⚽ EFL Championship play-offs: 2017 (Huddersfield Town)

*Excludes Super Cups

ZINEDINE ZIDANE

Zinedine Zidane was once the world's best player. As a coach he wants physically strong players, likes to have good team spirit, is happy to play a dull but effective style and is great at changing games with his substitutions.

NATIONALITY
French

CURRENT CLUB
Real Madrid

DEBUT YEAR: 2016

FIRST CLUB: REAL MADRID

CLUBS MANAGED	GAMES	LEAGUE TITLES
1	174	1

WINS	DRAW	LOSSES
114	37	23

CHAMPIONS LEAGUE TROPHIES	EUROPA LEAGUE TROPHIES	OTHER TROPHIES*
3	0	0

MAJOR CLUB HONOURS
⚽ UEFA Champions League: 2016, 2017, 2018
⚽ UEFA Super Cup: 2016, 2017
⚽ FIFA Club World Cup: 2016, 2017,
⚽ La Liga: 2017

*Excludes Super Cups

Printed and bound in Dubai
Author: David Ballheimer
Editor: Suhel Ahmed
Designer: Rockjaw Creative
Design Manager: Matt Drew
Picture research: Paul Langan
Production: Sarah Cook

All facts and stats correct as of May 2020

PICTURE CREDITS
The publishers would like to thank the following sources for their kind permission to reproduce the pictures in this book.